SPIRITUAL READING OF
NOVEL CORONAVIRUS
INFECTION ORIGINATED IN
CHINA

CLOSING IN ON THE REAL CAUSE OF THE GLOBAL OUTBREAK

RYUHO OKAWA

HS PRESS

Contents

5 Diseases and Disasters Urge People to Self-Reflect

6 A Message for Japan

Part II

The Global Situation in 2020 and the Warning Against a Hegemonic Nation

Chapter 1

Metatron's Message – UFO Reading 41 –

Chapter 2
R.A. Goal's Message
– UFO Reading 42 –

Chapter 3

Spiritual Messages from the Guardian Spirit of President Moon Jae-in and Yaidron

Afterword

Preface

Since the coronavirus originated in Wuhan, China, there have been over 40,000 infected cases and 900 deaths according to today's morning paper (February 11.)

We have made considerable updates in the last few days of the numbers within this book, but the level of disturbance this virus is causing has already exceeded that of the SARS outbreak. The cities of Wuhan and Beijing broadcasted on TV appear barren. Not limited to China, there has been a deficiency of masks even in Japan.

Prophesying misfortune leaves us with a bad feeling, so I have kept quiet until now. But I think the time has come for Happy Science to present its views, so I've decided to publish this book urgently. Indeed, a spiritual reading of a world unknown to you has been conducted.

Today is National Foundation Day in Japan. I can only pray that good comes out of bad.

Ryuho Okawa
Master & CEO of Happy Science Group
Feb. 11, 2020

Part I

Spiritual Reading of Novel Coronavirus Infection Originated in China

*Originally recorded in Japanese on February 7, 2020
at Special Lecture Hall, Happy Science, Japan
and later translated into English*

Interviewers from Happy Science[*]

Jiro Ayaori

Managing Director
Director General of Magazine Editing Division
Chief Editor of *The Liberty*
Lecturer at Happy Science University

Tesshu Saito

Senior Managing Director Overseeing the Editorial Divisions
Advisor in Charge of Content Development of
Entertainment, Performing and Media Arts Course,
Faculty of Future Creation, Happy Science University

Motohisa Fujii

Executive Director
Special Assistant to Religious Affairs Headquarters
Director General of International Politics Division

The opinions of the spirit do not necessarily reflect those of Happy Science Group. For the mechanism behind spiritual messages, see the end section.

---

[*] Interviewers are listed in the order that they appear in the transcript.
Their professional titles represent their positions at the time of the interview.

1

An Overview of
The Novel Coronavirus Infection

The situation of
The novel coronavirus outbreak in China

RYUHO OKAWA

As you may know, the coronavirus is constantly in the news almost every day. The novel coronavirus that originated in China is causing a situation in which an infection leads to severe pneumonia and even death.

Happy Science deals with a wide range of issues and is an unusual religion that has even started researching on such diseases and the pathogens involved. During the SARS and MERS outbreaks, I believe our monthly magazine *The Liberty* wrote featured articles on the diseases and described the spiritual reasons behind these outbreaks and how they had to do with God's or heaven's will.

As of this morning on February 7, 2020, the number of coronavirus cases recorded in China is 31,161 and the death toll is at 636. The number of cases outside of China is about 300. There have been two deaths, one in the Philippines and the other in Hong Kong.

The numbers of people infected are 86 in Japan, 28 in Singapore, 25 in Thailand, 24 in Hong Kong, 23 in South Korea, 16 in Taiwan, 15 in Australia, and so on. The total number of countries and regions with confirmed cases is 28, including mainland China. The number of cases around the world is about 31,500 and the death toll is almost 640. But it takes a while for the numbers to come out, so this disease may have spread farther than we know. The number of cases and the death rate are overwhelmingly high in mainland China. But quite frankly, the rate of infection and death elsewhere are not so different from the common cold. I hear that in Japan, one person who was infected and hospitalized has recovered and is now discharged. It seems that the fatality rate is much lower outside of China.

The origin of the virus and its effects

Looking at the events leading up to now, the first case of pneumonia caused by unknown reasons was reported on December 8, 2019. Is this a coincidence*? On January 1, 2020, the seafood market thought to be where the virus originated was closed. On January 20, Chinese President Xi Jinping issued instructions to curb the spread of the virus. On January 23, Wuhan closed its airport and railway stations. And on January 27, China banned outbound international group

---

* Happy Science celebrates its "Commemoration for the Day of Conquering the Devils and Attaining Enlightenment" on December 8.

tours, which severely affected the tourism industry in many countries. The reason why the city of Wuhan was delayed in reporting the outbreak was because they were waiting for approval from the government, which led them to expose a flaw in their system. They were unable to publicize such unfavorable news without government approval. The city and the state are going back and forth with each other over who is to blame.

There are over 50 different strains of coronaviruses, but only six of them can infect people. Of the six, two cause severe pneumonia. In the past, the viruses caused the SARS and MERS outbreaks.

There have been four charter planes sent from Japan to Wuhan to evacuate Japanese nationals. Also, the passengers of the luxury cruise ship anchored off Yokohama have not disembarked, and this is causing the coronavirus infection to spread among the onboard passengers (at the time of this recording).

The financial loss to China's tourism industry is estimated to be worth about ¥16 trillion (about US$150 billion). China's GDP growth between January and March of this year is expected to drop to less than 5 percent. Japan's GDP is predicted to fall by 0.2 percent as inbound consumption slows. It is reported in South Korea that some companies are being forced to suspend all of their factory operations.

Various causes of the outbreak

Objectively speaking, with one to two million people in Hong Kong demonstrating on the streets since last summer, the situation is very much like a civil war, so I wouldn't be surprised if people's thoughts manifested into reality and caused "something" to happen. Furthermore, since Ms. Tsai Ing-wen won the Taiwanese presidential election this January, I believe the

Beijing government would have been taking steps to intimidate Hong Kong and Taiwan from as early as January if nothing had happened. Amidst these conditions, the outbreak occurred as a counter to China's plans and forced them to deal with this domestic problem. Beijing may be secretly wanting to put up the "Great Wall" around Beijing to prevent the coronavirus from infiltrating the city.

I wish to investigate the causes of this outbreak today, but it is unclear how much will be uncovered. However, there is no doubt that a virus exists; a virus has emerged and is spreading.

One potential cause within China is the possibility of something being carried out of, leaked from, or involved in an accident at the rumored bacteriological weapons research lab in the Wuhan area. However, they would never publicize such incidents. Another country with bacteriological weapons is North Korea. I don't know how North Korea would benefit from causing this outbreak, but if they were curious to test out the power of one of their weapons, we cannot rule them out completely. Since they cannot test these weapons in their own country, they could have decided to unleash the virus in China instead.

Another possible cause is the U.S. The impeachment proceedings against President Trump were underway when General Soleimani was killed in a U.S. drone strike in Iraq at the beginning of January. This drew a lot of attention, so it appeared as though he was trying to divert attention away from the impeachment case to rally the nation behind him. On the other hand, he had also placed the trade and tariff war with China on the backburner in December, so it made me wonder what he was going to do with that.

Then, the infection of coronavirus began spreading in China. The U.S. also possesses bacteriological weapons, and so they wouldn't have to fight an outright war. All they need is one or two people to set a trap with a suitcase packed with the virus and spread it. The CIA or military could do it if they wanted to. It is possible that, while attacking Iran by drone, they tested out a bacteriological weapon in China.

They knew that it would be catastrophic if they fought a conventional war (against China) in Hong Kong or Taiwan. I would imagine they have the brains to cause such a panic instead, so we cannot totally rule out this possibility.

But as it turns out, China is completely contained on the world map. Hong Kong and Taiwan are saying "No more China," so it may be difficult for people to travel into and out of China. Some countries have imposed a travel ban on Taiwan too because the World Health Organization (WHO) sees Taiwan as a part of the People's Republic of China. People in Taiwan are furiously protesting against this, saying that they are not the People's Republic of China. In

Hong Kong, the borders have been closed off, but the medical staff have gone on strike, which has created an optimal environment to start an independence movement in Hong Kong.

This is probably all quite different from what Xi Jinping intended. I think it is also ruining the Japanese prime minister's plans to make up for the drop in consumption caused by the 10 percent consumption tax hike that went into effect last autumn. Although he may have hoped for the economy to improve with increased tourism during the Chinese New Year and the Tokyo Olympics, this scenario seems to have been ruined at this point.

Or, maybe this is all coincidentally caused by a naturally occurring virus, just as the scientists would think. But I believe that something else, like an earthquake or a tsunami, would have happened if this epidemic had not occurred.

Spiritual reading on the spirit
Involved in the novel coronavirus infection
Originating in China

RYUHO OKAWA

So, although I don't know how much we will get to uncover, I would like to do a spiritual reading and identify what is behind the emergence, infection, and spread of the new coronavirus. I do not know how much can be made public. We might discover things that cannot be released to the public. I was told to "stay put" until yesterday evening when I was finally given the approval to go ahead with the investigation. And so, I will give it a try today.

That said, I don't know if "the real coordinator" will reveal themselves. Someone else might appear, but I am hoping that we will get some kind of explanation.

Then, I will now begin the spiritual reading of the novel coronavirus infection that originated in China.

[*Inhaling and exhaling deeply.*] If there is anyone who is playing a central role in the novel coronavirus epidemic which originated in China, please come to Happy Science and tell us what is going on.

If there is anyone with some kind of intent, purpose, expectation for certain results, or thoughts regarding the novel coronavirus infection in China, please come down. If there is someone who played a central role in the proliferation of the coronavirus, was involved in God's or heaven's will, or was involved in any other spiritual cause behind the spread of the novel coronavirus, please come down to Happy Science and tell us your true thoughts and intentions.

[*About 20 seconds of silence.*]

2

Behind the Scenes of
The Novel Coronavirus Emergence

One of the beings responsible for
The novel coronavirus outbreak

SPIRIT
OK…

AYAORI
Hello.

SPIRIT
[*Inhaling deeply.*] OK…

AYAORI
Today, the world is in sort of a panic over the novel coronavirus. But I believe humankind must find a way to deal with this outbreak. We

hope to hear about your thoughts and opinions on this.

SPIRIT

Is that so? I thought you needed me to speak because *The Liberty* magazine has a deadline to meet.

AYAORI

No, no. We still have some time until then. [*Laughs.*]

SPIRIT

Ah, I see.

AYAORI

Yes, but thank you for looking out for us.

SPIRIT

I thought you were nearing your deadline. The information I'm about to share would lose its value if it were to come out too soon.

AYAORI

OK, thank you. I just want to confirm, are you the main being involved in the spread of the novel coronavirus?

SPIRIT

Yes, you could say I am one of those responsible for it.

AYAORI

So, you are in charge?

SPIRIT:

Yes.

Why the epidemic is spreading at this time

AYAORI

Looking at how highly contagious this virus is, and also how it is wreaking havoc in mainland

China, I cannot help but feel there is a purpose behind this. Can you tell us about the intention and the thought behind why this epidemic has taken over China at this time?

SPIRIT
Well… If not now, greater harm would have been inflicted. So, it is true that we intended China to direct their focus on domestic matters.

AYAORI
Are you saying that there could have been greater damage outside of China?

SPIRIT
Yes. They were planning to attack.

AYAORI
To attack?

SPIRIT

Hong Kong could have become like Uyghur.
Taiwan could have turned into another Uyghur
or Tibet as well.

AYAORI

I see. So, were they taking concrete steps to
initiate an attack?

SPIRIT

They already had a plan of attack in place for this
year. They wanted to take hard-line measures.

AYAORI

I see. In regards to Hong Kong, demonstrations
have been going on for over six months since
last year, while Ms. Tsai Ing-wen was reelected
in January in Taiwan. Are these the reasons for
timing this epidemic?

SPIRIT

There is a very deep meaning behind this. When masks were banned in Hong Kong, demonstrators had to fight, but now there is a shortage of masks all across China. It is a big problem now.

I would like them to realize that there is a kind of "lesson" here. They need to recognize how inhumane the things they have been doing are. Now, people are desperate for face masks. [*Laughs.*]

AYAORI

Reportedly, there are several research facilities, such as the Wuhan National Biosafety Laboratory or the Wuhan Institute of Biological Products, that the virus may have leaked from. What are your thoughts on this? Do these facilities have something to do with the virus?

SPIRIT

Well… when something like this coronavirus spreads like wildfire across the nation and causes many to die, it is possible to make them realize how inhumane the act of using a biological weapon is.

Biological weapons could be used outside of the country or where there is opposition. The world will immediately know if nuclear weapons are used, so it's difficult for them to be used. But biological weapons are harder to trace. For this reason, they should be developing a lot of biological weapons. In places like Uyghur, where resistance against the state is strong, there are ways to use biological weapons to easily make people sick and die. They should have been researching this as well.

So, this is why the ruling circle must understand what happens when these kinds of weapons are used.

The cause of a mutation
In the novel coronavirus

SAITO

Based on Master Okawa's explanation, only a few out of roughly 50 types of coronaviruses can affect human beings. According to Happy Science members who are also doctors, coronaviruses are normally not so malignant and only a few particular kinds of coronavirus evolve and make people sick.

It seems that one of these has mutated into something very lethal. Was there human involvement in the making of this virus? Or was there a strong spiritual influence at work?

SPIRIT

If I describe it in human terms, a massive thought of "wanting to kill the enemy" was swirling. When it hangs heavily over the

Earth like a thick cloud, it can take effect even on a microbial level and cause it to become murderous and malignant. It can also happen during an influenza outbreak. Thoughts of resentment turn viruses malignant. In other words, such vibrations of negative thoughts have the power to turn them malignant. They become like evil or malicious spirits. The land was full of such thoughts. Sooner or later, there would have been some kind of an explosion.

SAITO
Do you mean to say that China was filled with these thoughts and desires to kill...

SPIRIT
Yes. Thoughts of a massacre.

AYAORI
Is this mainly the Communist party's...

SPIRIT

So, it's "the CPC (Communist Party of China) virus." This is clear.

SAITO

"The CPC virus"?

SPIRIT

Yes.

AYAORI

So, are you saying that the thoughts of the communist leadership wanting to kill, crack down on, and suppress are growing stronger and spreading?

SPIRIT

Yes. Even if such situations hadn't unfolded, they would ultimately have the option of using chemical weapons instead of biological ones. The world has seen these being used in the Middle

East. This too leaves very little evidence, but many people have died in great tragedy.

Mr. Trump's methods such as shooting short-range missiles are conspicuous. But there are many people who choose to attack in obscurer ways by using biological and chemical weapons. North Korea is also looking into how to use them. While using nuclear weapons would invite a quick counterattack, these chemical and biological weapons would allow them to rattle others by causing pandemonium.

Why the virus originated in Wuhan, China

AYAORI
It is commonly thought that the virus originated in a seafood market, but in actuality...

SPIRIT
No. It has nothing to do with it.

AYAORI
Nothing?

SPIRIT
Uh huh. That's a lie.

AYAORI
Oh.

SPIRIT
They made it up to explain in this-worldly terms, but there is no link to it at all.

AYAORI
How should we understand the origin of this virus? Was it from an American, North Korean, or Chinese biological weapons lab?

SPIRIT
Think about what was previously explained and observe the world situation, then you will know.

You have to be highly intelligent to execute a plan such as this.

SAITO
In Wuhan, there is a biosafety level 4 laboratory, known to be a top-quality laboratory even in the world...

SPIRIT
Yes.

SAITO
The laboratory is part of the Chinese Academy of Sciences and is called the Wuhan Institute of Virology. It is involved in researching biological weapons.

SPIRIT
Yes.

SAITO

If the virus is originating from the same area as the lab, does that indicate...

SPIRIT

This is the epicenter. There is a reason why they have so many sick people in this area that hospitals are running out of beds. So yes, the cause lies here.

SAITO

I thought the cause lied within China.

SPIRIT

The cause does lie within China. Just as an egg is cracked, a slight force from the outside may have been applied to expose the contents.

SAITO

I see. So, they were working on a biological weapon, but similar to a move in Aikido, a different intent was applied, resulting in something that was not what China intended.

SPIRIT
They need to rethink their understanding of sanitation. Basically, much of their research is focused on how to kill people, but they have not done enough research on how to prevent deaths. They need to see what happens when something like this permeates throughout society. Even so, we selected an area where the casualty would be minimal.

AYAORI
Minimal?

SPIRIT
Yes, they have something greater.

AYAORI
I see.

SPIRIT

They have an even worse biological weapon.

AYAORI

I see.

SPIRIT

They're researching a much more vicious and deadly one.

The reason why only the weak, Such as the elderly, are dying

SPIRIT

One can actually be cured of this coronavirus with enough physical strength. Those who are physically weak, such as the elderly and disabled, die first. This weapon was not developed solely for war, but was also made to deal with the aging population in China.

Since they will not be able to make every pension payment to the elderly, they need people who are above a certain age to die. The safest way to have such people die is death by illness. It is the same approach as the Nazi gas chambers. If people over 80 contract pneumonia from a viral infection and die, it will appear very natural.

SAITO
According to the data of the current disease, the symptoms seem to appear more frequently in the elderly and those who have other illnesses.

SPIRIT
I'm sure it does. That's correct.

SAITO
There are reports that babies and young children show symptoms less frequently, and that even if they do, the symptoms seem to be kept to a minimum.

SPIRIT

China is developing biological and bacteriological weapons to fight foreign countries, but as I said just now, they also need to deal with the aging population. They basically had a policy to limit couples to having just one child, so in an aging society, it means they will run out of funds to pay for people's pension. This is similar to Japan.

The retirement age is about 60 for men and about 50 for women. Or if the woman is in management, she has until about 55. After that, they retire and the pension must be paid, so it is necessary to have them die early.

In such a totalitarian nation, it is very convenient when everyone dies in this kind of epidemic disease because they can simply dig a big hole, burn, and bury them all together. People are treated the same way as birds.

SAITO

So, behind this disease is the Beijing government's intention to weed out their population?

SPIRIT

Yes, yes. This is also part of the research.

SAITO

So, it's not just an attack.

SPIRIT

Right. It can be used to attack others, but there are also plans for "internal use." They may also use it against the Uyghurs and other "noisy and rampant regions" such as Southern Mongolia or Hong Kong. If they use real missiles or bombers, they will come under tremendous criticisms from other nations, but if an operative sneaks in and spreads something like this...

Something different could have happened. If the virus had spread throughout Hong Kong, China could have closed its borders, only to lend a hand when Hong Kong sought help. They would enter Hong Kong under the pretext of aiding and gain control of the region in this way. We could have seen a different scenario take place.

3

A Single Viral Outbreak Can Push International Politics into Action

The decision to intervene was made
Based on the analyses of the entire Earth
By a tool that goes beyond AI

AYAORI

So, did the current infection spread as a result of your taking advantage of or setting up a trap against the initial intention of the Communist Party of China?

SPIRIT

I can't reveal the specifics of the tool, but we have a more accurate grasp of where everything is on Earth than Google Maps can cover.

AYAORI

Is that right?

SPIRIT

Yes. Our calculations go beyond AI in regards to that.

SAITO

I feel that this is similar to the Buddhist concept of "evil deeds cause bad results."

SPIRIT

Yes.

SAITO

The Chinese government has been researching biological weapons with the desire to kill people or with the anticipation of gaining the power to reduce the population of the nation, but now everything unexpectedly came back to bite them. Despite their hopes to reduce the elderly population, it was as if the opportunity was "set up" by someone else's intention rather than their own, and they were forced to realize the horror of a biological weapon.

SPIRIT

That's right. They cover up facts even if an accident happens. They will never announce it publicly. If it were a voluntary accident, even Wuhan City would also hide information from Beijing. However, we cannot be sure if the accident was really "an accident" or not. We can see that these things can happen.

AYAORI

You mentioned earlier that you know where everything is on Earth. Does that mean you are seeing things from far above? Like from outer space?

SPIRIT

I guess that's one way to describe it. Yes.

However, it is very rare for us to intervene. We only intervene when necessary.

You will know that the Hong Kong people with masks from now on are truly rich. Masks are becoming rather expensive.

AYAORI

They are getting expensive.

SPIRIT

Something must be done.

The Japanese government did nothing, while Europe and the U.K. barely did anything.

The U.S. was pressuring China with tariffs alone, and took some action regarding the issue in Hong Kong. However, much of it seemed too much like a bluff. Then they intervened with Iran, but the problem of what to do with China remained.

AYAORI

I see. So, you saw the total picture and decided that a move had to be made now.

SPIRIT

At the very least, Mr. Xi Jinping is now half dead.

China's tendency to undervalue human lives Needs to be exposed

SAITO

On January 28, Mr. Xi Jinping told the Director-General of the World Health Organization who visited Beijing that, "This epidemic is a devil, and we cannot let the devil hide."

SPIRIT

That's right. "The CPC virus" is a devil.

SAITO

[*Laughs.*] Mr. Xi said shamelessly that, "It is a devil," and that "the Chinese people are in the midst of a serious battle with the outbreak of the new coronavirus infection, which is a devil. We cannot let it hide." If you look at this from the perspective of good and evil, it is...

SPIRIT

If the coronavirus spreads in Beijing, I'm sure the virus would become a "true devil." And if Beijing cannot do anything about it, people are bound to explode with frustration. There is certainly enough frustration built up right now.

SAITO

Eleven million people in Wuhan City are now in complete lockdown.

SPIRIT

Actually, five million people have already escaped. So, this infection is, in fact, spreading all over the country. In the current situation, people are trying to avoid being found, so they are hiding and running away as best as they can. So, the number of infected people is much larger.

SAITO

According to the doctors, fevers usually occur early on with these types of illnesses. But this new coronavirus has a long incubation period, so it is difficult to tell if people are infected or to detect with medical tests. Furthermore, it takes time. For this reason, the virus continues to be passed on before the symptoms show.

Is there any reason to extend the incubation time?

SPIRIT

Another thing is that China itself undervalues human life and has little desire to save people through medical institutions. They tend to neglect the idea of hygiene and saving lives especially since their population is so large.

There is a need to expose this situation. We saw the need to teach them how unprepared they are in dealing with this situation.

"Coronavirus alone can move International politics"

AYAORI
Control of information seems to be the fundamental political approach of the Communist Party...

SPIRIT
Yes, information control. That's right.

AYAORI
They often carry out politics by "obscuring information and exercising authority when giving orders," but this time, everything backfired.

The first case of infection occurred at the beginning of December, but when a doctor disseminated the information on the web, he was punished for "spreading a hoax."

SPIRIT
Yes, yes, yes. That's right.

AYAORI
In the end, they finally admitted it after about a month and a half, but by this time, the infection had already spread too far.

SPIRIT
Yes. What is more interesting is that in the current situation, North Korea, which conducts trade almost exclusively with China, is becoming reluctant to accept imports from China and is on the verge of collapse.

South Korea was also relying on China so that they can blame Japan, unify the North and

South, and lead international politics in a more favorable direction, but now their foothold has been disintegrated.

The other day, I believe the guardian spirit of the president of South Korea briefly came, but he should be screaming for help by now (see Part II Chapter 3). If China stopped, all of their factories would stop functioning.

So, they are currently weighing their options. South Koreans who think they may not last if they don't form a good relationship with Japan are gaining strength, so the current government is being shaken. This is how international politics can shift with just one coronavirus outbreak.

The novel coronavirus epidemic is
The "first signal"

AYAORI

The foothold of these three countries is becoming unstable.

SPIRIT

Yes. Japan is also becoming unstable.

AYAORI

Oh.

SPIRIT

Next, Japan will also become unstable when the economy stalls.

This is something Master Okawa has already mentioned last December*, "A recession originating in China will influence Japan." The

---

* The author talked about this in his lecture, "To the Age of New Prosperity" given on December 17, 2019.

current situation is not the full extent of what will happen. This is just the beginning.

AYAORI

Beginning.

SPIRIT

This is all happening as a warning that a recession may come. There's still more, though.

Now, there are quite a few Japanese companies that are retreating from China and many Japanese people living there are also pulling out. Furthermore, Japan was intending to improve its domestic economy through the inbound of Chinese tourists. This situation includes a warning to Japan that the country must shift its economic structure into one that allows its domestic economy to sustain itself without relying on these things.

The Japanese factories in China will continue to retreat and pull out as long as this coronavirus remains rampant. In reality, these factories should be moved to the remote, underpopulated regions of Japan. Now is the time for this, but the current administration is not thinking about it.

Anyway, this is just being sent as the first signal, so there are still the second and third signals to be sent out.

4

Is There a "Vaccine" Against the Novel Coronavirus?

The immunity that fights off The novel coronavirus

AYAORI

Will other shocking things happen as the second and third signals?

SPIRIT

They will be something different.

AYAORI

Is that so?

SPIRIT

While the current epidemic is spreading, this situation will persist, but the second and third signals will still come.

AYAORI

Will the next warning be another disease, or something else, like the ground shaking? Is it likely that various things will happen?

SPIRIT

If you were to write the Old Testament yourselves, it would be as though God's curses were coming one after another.

AYAORI

Oh. Just like Sodom and Gomorrah?

SAITO

For example, would the next one come after this is declared over, like how SARS was declared so? Or, will we see a series of continuous blows? What kind of future do you predict will come?

SPIRIT

In any case, we will make sure the world dislikes China's current way of approaching matters.

About 80 percent of Japanese people dislike the Chinese ways already and only a little over 10 percent of people like them. Now, Japan is being encroached on because there is economic profit involved, but there are things that should and shouldn't be spread.

I mentioned that this is the CPC virus, but on the contrary, there is something called "faith immunity." You could develop immunity towards the disease if you have faith in God. You won't die.

AYAORI
You won't die.

SAITO
Does it have medical effects too?

SPIRIT
You will not die.

SAITO

Faith immunity can change the body.

SPIRIT

That is why the disease is prevalent among materialists.

SAITO

And that's why it's called the CPC virus...

SPIRIT

Yes. It is prevalent in materialists.

AYAORI

There are many different faiths. For example, the Christian faith or the Buddhist faith. In this case, is it more important to have an honest heart to believe in God?

SPIRIT

Well, when comparing groups of people who do not believe in God and those who do, it is clear which side to support. But if two groups that believe in God are fighting one another, things become more complicated.

In medieval Christianity, when the Catholics and the Protestants were fighting each other, plagues like the Black Death became rampant and both sides lost many lives. This made them realize that such a religious war must end. We have been involved in such situations too.

Now, this disease can be repelled by faith immunity. It will not spread too much to countries with faith.

AYAORI
So, this is true at the national level and on the individual level.

SPIRIT
That's right.

SAITO
Having faith will have a spiritual effect...

SPIRIT

The virus's malignancy weakens. Viruses are small, but in short, when evil thoughts dwell in a virus, it becomes like an evil spirit. In addition, it could also become more deadly.

Naturally, it is sad to see weak people die, but it also overlaps with the needs of the Communist Party of China. If you see the true intention of the government internally, you will see that they need to place greater value on human life. In short, China currently possesses the belief that it is fine to kill those with inferior genes while protecting the superior genes, much like what the Nazis believed.

I think they need to reconsider their ideas.

The mechanism behind the viral outbreak

SAITO

Xi Jinping seems to be getting cornered and has been reflecting a little more on their actions. The Chinese leaders have accepted and acknowledged their mistake in dealing with the novel coronavirus. This is supposedly an extremely rare occurrence. Would self-reflection change the bad attitude of the leadership and cure the disease too?

SPIRIT

Well, the Chinese leaders themselves are aging, so if they ever get the disease, it is highly likely they will die soon after, so I think they are scared. They are pretty old, so yes, it seems dangerous for them. If the disease takes over Beijing, it would be a disaster, so they may be wanting to build the Great Wall around Beijing to prevent the spread. In this case, China's territory would become extremely small.

AYAORI

You mentioned that this virus is a CPC virus and is becoming more malignant because of the materialistic ways of thinking. Happy Science has been revealing the evil and demonic spiritual beings influencing China, so is it correct to think that these evil powers are causing the virus to become malignant?

SPIRIT

Umm, it's a bit difficult to do with your level of technology.

Originally, the attacking thoughts of China were supposed to be realized in various forms, like a horde of locusts heading towards Hong Kong, Uyghur, Taiwan, Japan, and other countries in Asia as well as the Middle East, Europe, and Africa. This spiritual current was flowing out, so we… oh, I wasn't supposed to say this… blocked it and confined it within.

AYAORI

Oh, I see. You created a state where the current is trapped and is whirling around in circles.

SPIRIT

That's right. To say it in terms which you would understand, we have created a type of spiritual screen.

AYAORI

Oh, I see. A barrier is formed, and the energy is contained.

SPIRIT

We are currently showing you how to "contain China."

China's violation of human rights is Reaching a level which even God or Buddha cannot forgive

FUJII

As you just said, objectively and from a global perspective, the Communist Party of China is being quarantined or isolated...

SPIRIT

Yes, they are certainly being quarantined.

FUJII

Yes. That seems to be the situation. However, as I listen to you, I am feeling that this is all happening based on a very clear will or intention.

SPIRIT

Yes, there is a clear intention.

FUJII

Did you choose this timing?

SPIRIT

Actually, we imagined that if we didn't act now, the spiritual current of their evil thoughts would conversely advance and attack various places by riding the tide of expansion. They were clearly planning on it because they could recover from their domestic economy stalling if they gain some foothold in other countries. If we had not taken action, it would have been the opposite outcome. There would have been various territories of different nations on fire while people ran about trying to escape.

FUJII

You mentioned earlier that you are looking at the Earth from a higher perspective. From your point of view, do you feel that China is the main focus right now? From an international political standpoint, there have been incidents in Iran as well, but do you still feel that China is what we should concentrate on now?

SPIRIT

The Middle East is going to be a big problem from here on out, so we understand that dealing with this is a separate issue.

However, the dangers in Hong Kong and Taiwan were approaching. Hong Kong, Taiwan, and China's domestic problem as well. The human rights violation within the country has become quite a big problem.

If it is difficult even for the U.S. to interfere, or if the U.S. can only interfere by intimidating them with tariffs, that means they could get away with anything as long as they control the flow of information.

So, for example, we currently do not know if there are three million people, two million people, or one million people being confined in the Uyghur concentration camps. China also looks up all the family members of the people who are participating in opposition movements abroad and are targeting their families thoroughly. The fact that these things are being done openly in a country that makes up one-fifth of the world's population means they have reached a level that even God or Buddha cannot forgive. The time to remove the lid and expose the contents is...

AYAORI
The international community, including Japan, has to urge China to disclose what is happening now and make everything clear.

SPIRIT
They will have to. At the next stage, rescue aid from foreign countries will come into China, which is what they fear the most. There is a shortage of hospitals in China because they lack the intention and motivation to save people. They don't have enough doctors, they easily abandon people, and they prescribe a ton of wrong medication or expired medication. There have also been countless medical errors that took place. We need to make China disclose all of this.

As foreign rescue aid enters,
The actual situation of China will be revealed

AYAORI

In the case of the former Soviet Union, after the Chernobyl nuclear plant accident occurred, Mikhail Gorbachev adopted "glasnost" as their slogan and decided to disclose information, which consequently led to the collapse of the regime. It seems China is being forced to go through a similar situation.

SPIRIT

China is highlighting their economic success and controlling the flow of information completely to prevent the dissemination of any negative impressions of China, so that they can demonstrate how well they're doing to the rest of the world.

But now the media around the world is watching China. Xi Jinping is trying hard to make amends domestically, but looking at the situation in Wuhan, things are obviously out of his control.

AYAORI

Yes.

SPIRIT

Just as we see on TV, temporary buildings are being built with a number of excavators, but China's true wish would be to just dig a hole, throw the patients in with some gasoline, and burn them alive.

Since they can't do this while the world watches, they are pretending to hospitalize the patients. But as the situation worsens, other countries will come to aid China, and it will eventually run out of excuses to turn down the help. And when this happens, their true conditions will be revealed.

China did not develop a vaccine

SAITO

When a country develops biological weapons, vaccines are also made as countermeasures. Did China prepare such things this time?

SPIRIT

No, they didn't.

SAITO

Were they simply focused on reducing the population?

SPIRIT

Not only was China intending to reduce their large population, but they were also intending to decrease the population outside of mainland China. So, what they actually wanted to do is more like, hmm... If China were to fly an airplane above major Japanese cities at night and drop these biological weapons like bombs, the virus would spread in no time without being detected.

AYAORI

Now that there is no effective vaccine, would you say that the power of faith will become essential?

SPIRIT

It seems like the HIV vaccine is becoming a little more effective.

AYAORI

Yes.

SPIRIT

HIV weakens the immune system and causes people to die early, so the HIV vaccine would work on the coronavirus patients to some extent. If patients can strengthen their immune system, they may be able to fend off the coronavirus, but China doesn't have such a big supply of HIV vaccines anyway.

AYAORI

Based on the idea of cause and effect, it makes sense that the power of faith or the strength of the mind boosts the immune system and can defeat the virus.

5

Diseases and Disasters Urge People to Self-Reflect

Diseases such as AIDS are a warning Against undesirable trends

SPIRIT

In the 1980s, when HIV spread in the U.S., we sent the virus as a warning.

AYAORI

You sent the virus?

SPIRIT

Yes, we sent it. Initially, the virus was seen as something that spreads among homosexuals and people became very cautious of such homosexual tendencies. However, once people eventually realized that it can spread to both homosexual and heterosexual people, our original intent of the warning became obscure. In any case, when an undesirable trend grows, we unleash diseases like that.

AYAORI

So, are you saying this has been repeated throughout human history?

SPIRIT

Yes, we have done this many times. We've always done it. I believe it happens at least two to three times every hundred years. We were involved during the Spanish flu pandemic as well.

SAITO

It is said that over 20 million people, or even 50 million people, worldwide died due to the Spanish flu.

SPIRIT

Yes, it was right before World War I. We tried to spread the Spanish flu before the war started... The reason for causing the 'Spanish' flu was because it was meant to be a warning against the imperialistic invasions that had been spreading from that region for 500 years.

SAITO

The Spanish flu spread around the time of WWI and over tens of millions of people died. There was also the plague...

SPIRIT

That's right.

SAITO

There were about 24 million people who died in Europe during the plague in the 14th century. The plague is also known as "the Black Death," but were you involved in this too?

SPIRIT

At that time, there were many witch hunts and witch trials, where people were burned alive and many heresy trials were conducted. These were unforgivable and abominable actions in a religious sense. It was a time when people couldn't tell the difference between good and bad religions. That is why the plague was sent down to warn people and to make them realize their mistakes.

AYAORI

So, this incident was also a result of bad thoughts created by people…

SPIRIT

That's right.

AYAORI

…that came back to bite them.

SPIRIT

As a result, the virus becomes malignant. When the amount of these bad thoughts increases to a certain extent, it starts to overflow as if a dam has been broken and spreads in some form or another. It will spread when it does.

SAITO

In this case, then, are powers from a higher dimension being used to surround and confine the virus inside China?

SPIRIT

That is one option. In the case of Columbus, he and his crew members contracted syphilis in the West Indies from the indigenous people and carried the virus back with them. It didn't take 100 years for it to spread across the world.

To explain this in a modern way, such incidents happened to teach that inhumane acts such as racism and rape are unforgivable. It was also meant to teach the importance of preserving chastity and a healthy family lifestyle, but unfortunately, syphilis spread around the world without the true lesson being realized. It spread as far as the British Royal family.

This situation will last until
The Chinese people sense heaven's will

AYAORI

Especially in the case of China, it has always followed a pattern where an infectious disease emerged and spread towards the end of a dynasty, when politics became corrupted and people began to suffer, and before a new regime arose.

SPIRIT

No matter how materialistic Chinese people have become, they have not forgotten that a revolution starts with heaven's will. So, we intend to keep this going until they become aware of heaven's will. However, spreading this coronavirus around the world isn't our intent.

AYAORI

I see.

SPIRIT

But we do not intend to stop this until Chinese people realize that the problem may lie within mainland China. If this prolongs, it could affect the Tokyo Olympics. But we don't care about the kind of economic effect the Tokyo Olympics would have, so I'll leave that up to you to deal with.

Hong Kong and Taiwan
Would have been in flames
If the infection had not caused a disturbance!?

SPIRIT

We have to do this now. You don't want to see Hong Kong and Taiwan up in flames, do you?

AYAORI

Are you saying that they were actually anticipating such a situation?

SPIRIT

China was preparing for that. They were preparing.

AYAORI

I see.

SPIRIT

Even with Hong Kong, it could have been possible for bombings and missile launches to start immediately with a single "GO" signal.

AYAORI

I recently read somewhere that the wages of the Chinese military officers suddenly increased around the end of last year. So, there have been various preparations going on.

SPIRIT

It was an "allowance for danger."

AYAORI

Ah, an allowance for danger.

SPIRIT

And probably "hush money."

AYAORI

Ah, hush money.

SPIRIT

Yes.

AYAORI

I see. So, are their preparations mostly ready?

SPIRIT

China believes they must act swiftly before the U.S. takes any military action. The U.S. is dealing with the Iranian issue now, so China may think that they are focused on that, but this could be part of Trump's strategy.

AYAORI

I see.

SPIRIT

China may think that the U.S. won't have time to deal with them because the U.S. would be preoccupied with the Iranian issue for a while. There is a chance that the U.S. is luring China's true intentions to surface.

AYAORI

Luring…

SPIRIT

Now that Trump's impeachment trial is over, I think he's going to make a move. His real intentions may be different.

AYAORI

I see.

SPIRIT

Yes.

AYAORI

Hmm. So, the U.S. is keeping a close watch on China.

SPIRIT

They intend to do so, but there is a chance they are involved with Iran as part of a diversion.

AYAORI

I see. I understand.

The effects on welcoming Xi Jinping
As a state guest

FUJII

You have a very good understanding of what's going on in the world now...

SPIRIT

Yes.

FUJII

We, the Japanese, will be welcoming Xi Jinping as a state guest in the spring. Japan had no plan against this. Do you have any thoughts on these matters?

SPIRIT

One excuse is to keep the virus out of the Imperial Palace, assuming the outbreak lasts until April.

Our hope and intent
Towards greater disclosure of
Information and democratization

AYAORI

You said that it is not your intention to spread the virus so much outside of China, but even so, I think each country needs to come up with ways to respond and deal with the virus. Is there anything we can do to help reduce innocent people from getting infected or dying?

SPIRIT

Usually, people dying isn't considered as such a good thing, so you may think it's all evil. Right now, the elderly and disabled people are dying first, but these are people who will eventually be killed by the Chinese government.

It's just a matter of time, and when the Chinese economy declines they will all be killed. They would all be on the death list. China lacks the ability to save them nor do they have the capacity to hospitalize them. We are trying to spread awareness on this matter ahead of time.

We are trying to make China understand that they need to improve their medical field and treat their people better. We want to start a movement where the government can disclose information accurately especially when it is unfavorable for the people.

So basically, as El Cantare* says, we are trying to encourage the Taiwanese and Hong Kongese way of thinking to prevail over China. This is one way of going about it.

---

* The Supreme God of the Earth Spirit Group; God of the Earth who has guided humanity since the beginning of Earth and who was also involved in the Creation of the universe. See Ryuho Okawa, *The Laws of the Sun* and *The Laws of Faith* (both New York: IRH Press, 2018).

AYAORI

So, do you mean that a democratic movement like the one in Hong Kong will begin to occur simultaneously in mainland China as well?

SPIRIT

It's an opportunity to start a movement, yes. Without it, small movements have no chance against Great China. But now, more than 60 countries are reluctant to allow Chinese people to enter their country. They are rejecting trade, commerce, investments, and contracts from China. They are even rejecting group tours.

The Chinese government takes advantage of Chinese tourists as a diplomatic strategy. For example, China sends many people to various islands and tourist spots for sightseeing and encourages the construction of more infrastructure in these places. They even lend money to have the infrastructure installed, but once the tourists return to China, the tourism locations can no longer repay the debt and are forced to beg and "pay respect to Beijing".

China has been cultivating and taking advantage of such relationships for a long time. They must have been using the same strategy with Japan as well. So now, we are trying to stop them from continuing.

The intent to change the cultural spheres Of China, North Korea, and South Korea

SAITO

On January 30, Master Ryuho Okawa saw the situation and bestowed upon us a ritual prayer called, "Prayer for Defeating the Infection of Novel Coronavirus Originated in China." And in the prayer, it says, "El Cantare, / Under Your name, / Save those who believe in You. / Just urge China to self-reflect."

SPIRIT

Yes, yes.

SAITO

There is a goal to urge China to self-reflect. What do you think of this?

SPIRIT

Fundamentally, they cannot reflect on themselves. This is true of the Chinese, but also the North Koreans and South Koreans.

If this tendency in this cultural sphere doesn't change, they will become the "cancer cells of Asia" in the future. Not only are they incapable of self-reflection, but they also fabricate lies. They make up fake history and pressure others to self-reflect. They then demand compensation and take the money from you. They possess such tendencies.

From your perspective, this is similar to how gangs operate. The people of China, North

Korea, and South Korea all have this cultural gene in common.

SAITO

That's true. They have done all kinds of things since this outbreak, like concealing the facts and falsifying data to reduce the number of infections. This happened during the SARS outbreak too. There are quite a few lies involved. The same goes for South Korea as well. Do you intend on changing this "culture of lying"?

SPIRIT

When the Soviet Union was still around, the Berlin Wall fell after the Cold War, and the northern side collapsed. North Korea needs a similar ending to their dictatorship, much like what Romania experienced under Ceausescu. Such a country shouldn't be allowed to keep going, so we intend on bringing an end to it.

Natural disasters are also expected
To occur in America

AYAORI

Do you mean to bring an end to those regimes within the next few years?

SPIRIT

There is more to come, so this won't be the end. There are problems between Israel and Islamic countries, conflicts among Islamic countries, the EU problem, and Russia's potential rise to prominence again. So, there are many complicated factors at hand.

The United States has issues as well. If we are not careful, there is a chance they might become like the ancient Baal religion. They are starting to measure happiness and faith in terms of money.

AYAORI

Does that mean President Trump also has that tendency?

SPIRIT

I can't say that he doesn't. Because he possesses such qualities, it's unclear what will come about in the future. The Democratic Party is headed towards dangerous territory. The U.S. is about to sink to the bottom of the Pacific from the West Coast, where their westward movement reached. It means U.S. liberalism is about to come to an end.

Unless the people who believe liberalism is democracy adopt new ways of thinking, there is a chance for their civilization to end.

AYAORI

Do you mean there'll be something like a natural disaster?

SPIRIT

Yes. Especially on the West Coast. We can expect a considerable number of natural disasters on the American West Coast.

AYAORI

A considerable number?

SPIRIT

Yes. By that, I mean a series of them. And this is because their way of thinking is… It simply means that mistaken ideas are spreading there.

A multi-layered plan is currently
In the works

SAITO

A decade ago, Master Okawa summoned the spirit of Edgar Cayce*, who said that an unknown disease would deploy its legion in the next decade. This year marks exactly 10 years since then. Does that mean you'll bring about more illnesses and natural disasters to encourage change?

---

* The author recorded "Future Reading by Edgar Cayce" on October 6, 2010.

SPIRIT

In regards to basic human rights, China is... I wish to destroy their totalitarian system that brainwashes people with lies.

In terms of the U.S., their approach to human rights should not go too far in the opposite sense. They should not be willing to turn their backs against God's will even if it means being kind to people. It is also unforgivable for human freedom to become so almighty that it allows people to do whatever they please.

Regarding the Islamic regions, their strict adherence to rules that were created over 1,000 years ago is taking away the possibilities of many people and is causing much suffering. Ideas that lead to terrorism also exist in their ideology. So they need to disclose information and need to change and become a country that upholds freedom of thought, expression, and action, as well as the freedom to vote for their own leaders.

There are various "time gaps" around the world where a multitude of governing systems are in place. We are in the process of creating a multi-layered plan to pull these systems closer towards a more ideal direction.

6

A Message for Japan

"Japan will also face a situation
In which they must reflect on"

FUJII

Are you aware of any issues regarding the current state of Japan?

SPIRIT

Regarding Japan, it's quite awkward for me to say this, but it's about time the country woke up. Even though the Great Hanshin Earthquake and the Great East Japan Earthquake occurred, the leftists only got stronger, and the country continued to apply a fiscal stimulus, thereby making the country weaker.

Japan needs to "clean up" their defeat in WWII, the half-hearted preservation of the

Imperial system, and the relationship between true faith and the Imperial system, which is to say, the relationship between the existence of God and Buddha and the Imperial system. The clean-up is just starting.

Japan experienced major changes in the Meiji Restoration, but they also abandoned religious faith at the same time. So, instead of worshiping God or Buddha in heaven, they had a system that enshrined the emperor as a living god instead of a king on earth. As a result, they lost the war.

The emperor is a being who should enlighten the people by communicating with the Japanese gods in Takamagahara or the universal God through ritual practice. So, it is not ideal for him to exist as a mere substitute for God without expounding any teachings. It will be good if the preservation of the Imperial family means that Japan would prosper as a religious nation. However, this has not been the case for some time now.

And democracy within the governing system also seems to be decaying a little. For example, when a Japanese opposition party briefly asked in the Diet about why the Happy Science University was not approved as a university, the Ministry of Education, Culture, Sports, Science and Technology (MEXT) said things like, "There was fraudulent conduct," and "There's a problem with the dean." It sounded to me like they basically didn't feel obligated to support it because Happy Science has a political party.

The opposition party should have retorted by saying, "Are we correct to understand that you will not approve any university established by a group that founded a political party?"

If the ministry had said yes, it would mean that these Diet members are not serving all of the people, but only those who are loyal to their party. They would be considering matters solely based on how advantageous these are for their party, which would mean that Japan's democracy is corrupt.

In reality, when the same party stays in power, they become focused on their own interests and begin to defeat other parties, become ministers and attain power. Some may even try to maintain their power at the cost of creating a financial deficit. Lies and deception are left unchecked.

So, many responses from members of the Diet are full of lies, while the bureaucrats become experts of deceit.

While this is a governing system that was established after the Meiji Restoration, we are reaching a point where we need to clean it all up. Japan will experience a situation where people must reflect on themselves completely. Japan must prepare for this.

AYAORI
Do you mean for something like a natural disaster...

SPIRIT
That is also approaching.

AYAORI

OK.

SPIRIT

The issue with MEXT is that they still don't realize that they've received so much divine punishment. So, unless they realize it, something will continue to occur.

Disastrous conditions in China
Had been declared ahead of time

SAITO

On January 2 of this year, Master Ryuho Okawa contacted a space being who helps protect the Earth. The being relayed a message that said, "This is the year to drive a wedge into totalitarian nations." (See Part II Chapter 1)

And the other message was like a declaration that said, "The Chinese military is planning to attack Hong Kong, Taiwan, and the Senkaku

Islands, so we will take action from space as a threat to China and cause natural disasters that may even appear to be divine will." (See Part II Chapter 2)

SPIRIT
Yes.

SAITO
This happened on January 3. After the declaration was made, there was the novel coronavirus outbreak.

SPIRIT
Yes, yes. But it's just the beginning.

SAITO
So, this was scheduled...

SPIRIT
Yes.

SAITO

Does this mean you clearly intended for this to happen?

SPIRIT

Yes, that's exactly right. We knew Tsai Ing-wen would win. Japan has a mission to fulfill after that, but the nation is not prepared to do so.

Japan's overall faith is getting weaker and has regressed to the level of worshiping local deities for personal gain at best. No matter how many times Goddess Amaterasu warned them, they still don't understand. The Imperial family also needs to think more seriously about this. There should be a big spiritual vortex around them right now.

It is easy to tell you what will happen to Japan, but it is better not to do so now. So, I will refrain from commenting. But when that thing does happen, the mass media will probably interpret it in the opposite way as they always do, so please know that you will need to guide them in the correct direction with precise arguments.

You have a mission.

The spirit reveals his name

FUJII

Regarding the spiritual message in January that was touched on in the previous question, the message on January 3 was from a space being called R.A. Goal*.

SPIRIT

Hmm...

FUJII

We would like to know if you are also a space being or maybe a spiritual being.

---

* A space being from Planet Andalucia Beta in Ursa Minor. One of the commanders of the space defense force. A certified messiah.

R.A. GOAL
Hmm… I am R.A. Goal.

FUJII
OK.

SAITO
OK… After you told us on January 3 that you'd cause a natural disaster, you also told us to keep a close watch on the world situation. Just as we were anxiously keeping watch, this happened, so it all started to make sense…

R.A. GOAL
Yes.

There is a "sequel" to the novel coronavirus Outbreak and a crisis approaching Japan

R.A. GOAL

But there's still more.

SAITO

There's more!?

R.A. GOAL

Yes. We are deciding how far to go with this, where to let it peak, and figuring out what to cause next. There's something waiting for Japan, too. I believe this has already been prophesied, but a crisis will occur in Japan as well.

SAITO

Can it take a different form?

R.A. GOAL

Yes. A crisis will come. And you will have to think about how to escape it, just like in the Exodus.

SAITO

You spoke about something like "faith vaccine" to combat the CPC virus, and how there is faith immunity...

R.A. GOAL

Well, if Japan receives divine punishment, it will be because they treated El Cantare too lightly. We can no longer allow this. We've reached our limit.

SAITO

However, in this world, when there is no scientific or man-made evidence, natural disasters tend to appear like natural phenomena, for example. It can be difficult to see that there is any divine intention involved. Are you urging people to figure out a way to self-reflect and sense it on their own?

R.A. GOAL

We will keep going until they can sense it.

SAITO

Will you really keep going until they can sense it?

R.A. GOAL

Yes.

SAITO

OK, I understand.

"We possess powers
Comparable to that of the Earth's saviors"

AYAORI

Earlier, you used the word, *we*.

R.A. GOAL

Haha! Haha!

AYAORI

Do you have a team of people cooperating?

R.A. GOAL

Well, I can't reveal everything.

AYAORI

OK.

R.A. GOAL

There are beings who can reveal themselves and those who cannot. Our strategy is for beings like Yaidron (See Part II Chapter 3) and myself to fight at the forefront. Some of us are still hidden.

AYAORI

I see.

R.A. GOAL

However, our powers... We, of course, possess powers comparable to that of the saviors of Earth. Please keep that in mind.

So, if you people no longer understand Moses's divine plagues and disasters, we're trying to make you understand what those occurrences would look like in the modern world.

We want you to know that we have the capability of doing anything.

There is a need to destroy
The "pro-Chinese gene" ingrained in Japan

SAITO

When Master Okawa recently visited Canada[*], there was a Q&A session at the lecture.

R.A. GOAL
OK.

SAITO

He elaborated on the true meaning of the Golden Age and explained that "It means, we

---

[*] The author held a lecture and a Q&A session in English titled, "The Reason We Are Here" in Toronto, Canada on October 6, 2019. See Ryuho Okawa, *The Reason We Are Here: Make Our Powers Together to Realize God's Justice - China Issue, Global Warming and LGBT* - (Tokyo: HS Press, 2020).

will destroy atheists or non-believers in God on this Earth, and such kind of great power will be ruined from 2020 to 2030. For example, it means the gigantic country which doesn't believe in God and is just one-party system and communism-only country, will be destroyed by dint of God's power."

R.A. GOAL
Yes.

SAITO
Is it correct to understand your activities as part of this plan?

R.A. GOAL
Yes, and in a way, Japan is also becoming like China. Don't you think? In a way. It's becoming like China and... They look up to China for their economic development and tend to flatter and copy them.

Right now, we are giving punishment to China, but Japan itself is now slowly heading towards totalitarianism.

We need to counter this by creating a properly functioning democracy where God's will can flow through as it should. But in the Diet, people lie and deceive others, so that they don't have to take responsibility. And while those who enforce laws should be impartial, they are being used to keep the political party in power. In a situation where the greed of these politicians who are supposed to stand above the citizens is being completely accepted by the public, we need to put a clear end to such problems.

You might feel powerless in all things, but there is a "pro-Chinese gene" that is ingrained in Japan. This cultural gene is prevalent in the mass media, the people, and the educational system. Particularly in academia, the idea that something can only be academic if it is materialistic and scientific is prevailing.

The Golden Age will not come unless we destroy these things.

7

Earth is an Experimental Ground among The Messiah Planets in Space

The evil gods of the universe are Attempting to spread Chinese values

FUJII

Various powers are at work as part of the intervention from space against the materialistic country of China. How should we on Earth understand the meaning behind the fact that you are sending us messages while revealing your name?

R.A. GOAL

There are enemies out there, too.

FUJII

Yes.

R.A. GOAL

There are enemies from outer space. They can attack as well.

FUJII

Are there space people lending their powers to China too?

R.A. GOAL

Yes, there are. It's a war of wits.

FUJII

OK.

R.A. GOAL

In the end, we are the mainstream and we are the ones who have been guiding the Earth for a long time, so we need to completely block the tactics of those who are intervening for the purpose of invading.

AYAORI

We've been taught about Kandahar and Ahriman, and understand them as the evil gods of the universe...

R.A. GOAL

They are also intervening.

AYAORI

What are they currently thinking about?

R.A. GOAL

They're trying to put key locations under their control based on Chinese values. "Erasing Japan from the world map by 2050" is one of their ideas. From their perspective, Hong Kong and Taiwan should have already been erased from the map a long time ago.

The reason why the spiritual reading
On the novel coronavirus outbreak
Was permitted now

AYAORI

In the opening comments, Master Okawa spoke about "getting the green light" on investigating the coronavirus the day before (February 6, 2020)…

R.A. GOAL

Yes, I gave the green light at 6 pm yesterday.

AYAORI

OK. What would you say is the meaning of this?

R.A. GOAL

Well, your magazine deadline is…

AYAORI

Ah, no, no, no. [*Audience laughs.*] Let's put that aside for now. [*Laughs.*]

R.A. GOAL

Haha. I think it's getting a little too late for it to be news. It needs to be released soon.

AYAORI

Yes.

R.A. GOAL

So, it's actually better for us to operate under the radar, since we could be met by resistance.

AYAORI

Oh, right. They will make a different move, correct?

R.A. GOAL

Yes, they'll counter our move. Since that is how it is… We need to do things in secret, which is why we delayed our signal for a few days. But I thought it should be OK by now.

This case could last for a while longer. I think it could be drawn out to around March or April. After this, we have something else planned.

SAITO

In that case, President Xi Jinping won't be able to visit Japan…

R.A. GOAL

Whatever happens, we'll make sure it's newsworthy.

The relationship
Between R.A. Goal and El Cantare

SAITO

There are many sacred beings and high spirits on Earth, including Buddha. Are you cooperating with these saviors as you make your moves?

R.A. GOAL

(El Cantare) has broken into the realm of space, so, to be honest, He is beyond the level of Earth's saviors. He is beyond it. So, Earth is actually an experimental ground that is attracting much attention among other Messiah Planets in space.

SAITO

A moment ago, you expressed your opinion towards those who don't agree with El Cantare's thoughts and how you can no longer allow them to look down on or not recognize the existence of El Cantare.

In this case, does that mean that those who possess greater powers than Earth's sacred beings and messiahs maintain such perspectives and still protect El Cantare?

R.A. GOAL
Actually, we were the ones who received guidance.

SAITO
Oh, so you received El Cantare's guidance.

R.A. GOAL
Yes, a long time ago. We have received guidance in the past.

SAITO
Wow…

R.A. GOAL
We received guidance, and now we work to guide other planets.

Only 30 percent of the Laws of El Cantare Have been revealed

R.A. GOAL

Only around 30 percent of the teachings have been revealed. The other 70 percent haven't been revealed yet. You need to make more progress in your work for the rest of the Laws of El Cantare to be revealed.

SAITO

There's still 70 percent left?

R. A. GOAL

That is what hasn't been revealed.

SAITO

It's been over 30 years since the first law was expounded on...

R. A. GOAL

Yes. Only around 30 percent have been revealed.

SAITO

Huh…

R. A. GOAL

In order to reveal the other 70 percent, Happy Science has to spread further and become recognized. That's why we're in a hurry and we're trying to adjust it.

Since we haven't reached that point yet, we need to make sure the Laws of El Cantare will be fully revealed. Unfortunately, the disciples are too slow and they are being obstructed a lot by the existing influences of the Japanese public, mass media, and other powers overseas.

8

Now is the Time for a Revolution To Establish the World of "Freedom, Democracy, and Faith"

"If China becomes a hegemonic nation, You will be regarded as 'livestock'"

SAITO

As we approach the end of the session, I'd like to ask a question about human rights. You spoke about countries that downplay the value of human life earlier. El Cantare has taught us that we're all children of God. As such, is it correct to assume that you don't want a country that downplays human life to expand and progress?

R. A. GOAL

Yes, but that's not all. You must have faith, and it must be based on the Truth. It's desirable for people who have faith based on the Truth to prosper in this world. We'd be in trouble if the world were rampant with people who are like mold.

If the population heading towards 10 billion becomes atheist, materialist, or they start to worship AI like a god, we would have to destroy such a world. That would be our only option. We are currently rushing, so that we can stop such an outcome from happening.

So, just think about what would happen to you if China becomes a hegemonic nation and starts controlling the world with surveillance cameras and AI. You will all become livestock.

SAITO
Livestock?

R. A. GOAL
Yes, you will be treated as "human livestock."

Democracy presumes that each individual Possesses the life of God within

SAITO

Master Ryuho Okawa teaches the importance of "freedom, democracy, and faith" in a democracy that acknowledges the existence of God. Do you have any guidance for us in realizing such a future vision?

R. A. GOAL

A sufficient headcount does not determine the legitimacy of a democracy. If this were true, the People's Republic of China would also be a democracy because I'm sure they consider themselves the People's "Democratic" Republic of China. However, we are not talking solely about the number of heads, but rather about each person being given a life of God, and possessing goodness within them. That is why each person has one vote and one opinion.

Without this depth of understanding, you will regress to the time when modernization began in the 17th and 18th centuries, such as the development of philosophy, science, and art, and lose the spirituality that humans possess. This will result in the birth of many superficial people.

In some ways, this will be a big actualization of the "Noah's Ark" phenomenon. But we want Japan and the world to correct their ways before it gets to that point.

AYAORI
Thank you.

Now is the time for a revolution in China, A country built on corruption and lies

AYAORI
As our final question, we'd like to ask about understanding God... When diseases and natural

disasters occur, people on Earth may see them as a cause of great unhappiness and many may begin to hate God. For those who feel this way, would you explain how they should understand God?

R. A. GOAL

In places like China, where the population is huge and economic progress is upheld as their slogan especially in recent times, people think that as long as they become wealthy through economic progress, this world is heaven and that they don't need God or Buddha.

But on the contrary, basic human morals and values are imperative. It's good for people with such values to have economic freedom, freedom to travel, or the freedom of occupation. But if a fundamental aspect is missing and only a small group of people have great power, it will definitely lead to the creation of a distorted world. The only condition under which China is allowed to influence the world is that China itself nurtures many people who uphold values worthy of leading the world. They were once a country that nurtured many great people especially during their prosperous era, so if China can be that way, they should be allowed to influence the world. But right now, there is nobody great in China. The country is all caught up in Mao Zedong's totalitarian thought.

A country founded by someone who has now become a devil in hell should not be allowed to prosper for such a long time. It may feel like China is prospering, but that's only because people haven't realized that Mao Zedong is a devil.

This is something we need to make clear. Mao Zedong is a devil. We need to clarify what he did and let the people of China and the world know about it. They say the Japanese army is all to blame, but I'm sure that's not the case. The countless horrors they've committed after the founding of their country may even surpass what Nazi Germany did. A country built on corruption and deceit is a house of cards. It shouldn't continue to prosper. There is a need to destroy it once, make them self-reflect, and recreate the foundations.

This is the time for a revolution. I think now is the time.

AYAORI
We will stand up to fight for the revolution. Thank you.

We can stop time
In the case of a sudden threat

R. A. GOAL
We also protect Japan from outside enemies.

SAITO

Thank you.

R. A. GOAL

We protect you from things that may not be defendable by the Self-Defense Forces PAC-3, so you can trust us on that point. While this is impossible at your level of technology, we can basically stop time with ours. We can stop time in the case of a sudden threat, so we can make adjustments during that time.

I think you can rest assured in this regard.

If you explore the meaning of religion, You will reach the core Truth of the universe

R. A. GOAL

However, only around 30 percent of the teachings have been revealed and they have not been spread wide enough. They haven't reached enough people in the world nor within Japan. If things end here, Happy Science will be remembered briefly as one of many post-war religions in Japan and will be soon forgotten.

This is mainly because the level of enlightenment among the disciples is still low. You need to reach a deeper understanding of the true meaning of religion.

It's important to understand that pursuing the meaning of religion will eventually lead to the mysteries of the universe and the core Truth of the universe. These are also what El Cantare wants to teach, but you don't have a big enough capacity to receive such teachings yet. You must understand this.

AYAORI
Yes.

R. A. GOAL

Anyway, we'll try to keep things "busy" this year, so that *The Liberty* constantly has material to write about.

AYAORI

Thank you [*laughs*]. We'd be honored. First, we will make sure to awaken ourselves.

R. A. GOAL

If you feel satisfied when 5,000 or 10,000 people listen to Ryuho Okawa's opinions, that is not enough. His words carry more importance than the front-page article in a newspaper. I'm saying, your culture of not being able to perceive important things as important indicates how low your level is. I'm telling you to be enlightened. If the disciples can't understand this, how can you expect others to do the same?

AYAORI

Yes. We'll make sure to consider this seriously.

Trying to teach China to look at Where they are

R. A. GOAL

I told you about who the central being behind the coronavirus is. But this isn't done independently by me alone. It also includes an aim to reveal the fact that China is researching bacteriological weapons.

Furthermore, there is a need to make known their lack of respect for human lives. How can a country that treats its own people this way hold responsibility for people of other countries? They will only plague these people like a swarm of locusts. We're trying to tell China to watch where they are.

Unfortunately, several hundred people have died within a population of 1.4 billion, but there is no need to worry because we'll take care of them in the other world. It is easier for them to go to heaven if they die early. China is a country where the longer you live, the longer you'll have to stay in hell.

SAITO
OK, thank you.

R. A. GOAL
Are we all set?

SAITO & AYAORI
Yes.

R. A. GOAL
I'm one of many commanders, but I'd like you to understand the significance of expressing our opinions from space.

AYAORI

Yes. Thank you for today.

9

After the Spiritual Reading:
The Golden Age Will Begin with
Hardship and Suffering

RYUHO OKAWA

[*Clapping twice.*] So, there we go. The next strike won't come while this one is still spreading. When it stops spreading, however, the next…

SAITO

The next…

RYUHO OKAWA

Something else might start. "A lid" may be opened. We'll be busy this year.

AYAORI

We learned that this year will begin with hardship and suffering, after all.

RYUHO OKAWA

Yes, yes. I expected the Golden Age to begin with hardship and suffering. But this was anticipated because we're reversing a trend that is spreading across the world. So, the political systems, which aren't being questioned, need to change as well.

SAITO

We received *The Laws of Steel* (New York: IRH Press, 2020) from you this year. We'll study it thoroughly and move forward with much strength.

RYUHO OKAWA

OK. Thank you.

INTERVIEWERS

Thank you.

Part II

The Global Situation in 2020 and the Warning Against a Hegemonic Nation

It is said from ancient times that those who have attained enlightenment like Shakyamuni Buddha can use abilities beyond human knowledge freely at their will, namely the Six Divine Supernatural Powers (astral travel, clairvoyance, clairaudience, mind-reading, fate-reading, and spiritual wisdom). These spiritual abilities of the highest level transcend the boundaries of time and space, and enable one to freely see through the past, present and future lives. Okawa is able to use these Six Divine Supernatural Powers freely and conduct various readings.

In the spiritual reading sessions compiled in this book, Okawa uses these abilities to conduct spiritual messages, spiritual vision, time-travel reading (seeing through the subject's past and future), remote-viewing (sending part of the spirit body to a specific location and seeing the situation there), mind-reading (reading the subject's thoughts and will, including those in a remote location), and mutual conversation (communicating with the thoughts of various beings that are beyond human contact).

Chapter 1

Metatron's Message
– UFO Reading 41 –

*Originally recorded in Japanese on January 2, 2020
at Special Lecture Hall, Happy Science, Japan
and later translated into English*

Metatron

A space being from Planet Include in Sagittarius. A part of Jesus Christ's space soul (Amor). Born in Mesopotamia about 6,500 years ago. One of the gods of Light.

Interviewers from Happy Science[*]

Shio Okawa
Aide to Master & CEO

The opinions of the space being do not necessarily reflect those of Happy Science Group.

1

2020: The Year to Drive a Wedge Into Totalitarianism

Just like the year before, Metatron came to Say his "New Year's greetings"

RYUHO OKAWA

It is January 2, 2020, a little before 10 pm. Maybe…

SHIO OKAWA

Are we seeing it in the direction towards Shinagawa?

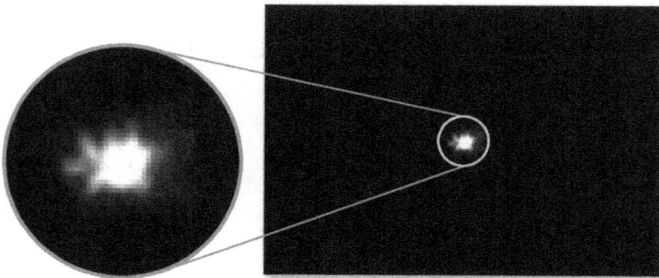

Metatron's UFO captured in this recording session
Spotted by Ryuho Okawa / Video taken by Shio Okawa
January 2, 2020 at 10:14 pm in Tokyo
(left: enlarged image)

RYUHO OKAWA

Yeah, it looks like it's in the sky above Shinagawa. Something that is emitting a strong light has appeared. There are many other stars in the sky, but unlike the others, I can sense some kind of a will in its light. So, this one is highly likely to be different from the rest.

I will now speak to it.

To the one that is currently emitting a strong light in the sky above Minato Ward. To the one emitting a strong light above Minato Ward. Are you an entity with a will that is different from a star?

[*About 5 seconds of silence.*]

* All texts in bold and quotation marks are the words of the space being that Ryuho Okawa conducted a reading on.

RYUHO OKAWA

It says, **"I've come to give my New Year's greetings."**

SHIO OKAWA

Which planet are you from?

RYUHO OKAWA

"Metatron. I'm sorry, I'm Metatron. You are starting the year with me again.*"

SHIO OKAWA

Yes. Thank you so much for looking after us last year.

RYUHO OKAWA

"I'm sorry. I've come to pledge that I will continue working hard again this year."

---

* When the author recorded a spiritual reading on a UFO on January 1, 2019, Metatron appeared and gave his New Year's greetings.

This year will be the deciding year of Whether a war will start or not

SHIO OKAWA

In the TV program, *Yarisugi Toshi Densetsu* (lit. "Urban Legends Gone Too Far"), they said Jesus Christ is a 'humalien'…

RYUHO OKAWA

"Hmm. Is that supposed to be a hybrid of a human and a space being?"

SHIO OKAWA

Yes.

RYUHO OKAWA

"We often operate in outer space, so I guess we are both. I'm sure El Cantare has work in other universes, too. I bet it's very difficult to tie everything together. His mission is beyond Earth indeed.

"I too am a part of this mission. Jesus Christ is currently giving guidance as an Earthling, but I also have connections to outer space*. Right now, my job is to guide Earth as well, so I am currently strengthening my powers."

SHIO OKAWA
Thank you.

RYUHO OKAWA
"We need to work hard again this year. We must keep strongly encouraging and supporting activities overseas. This year, we may or may not see the start of a war. The Tokyo Olympics is coming, too. On top of that, Japan's political situation is uncertain and there are two flashpoints in the Gulf and Asia. We should also be on the alert for Russia's next moves. We must properly manage all these matters."

---

* Translator's footnote: Metatron is a part of Amor, which is the space soul of Jesus Christ. Here, Metatron is saying that Jesus's main work is on Earth while Metatron himself is mainly involved with activities in outer space.

SHIO OKAWA

Yes.

RYUHO OKAWA

"If you have any questions, I will answer them as part of my New Year's greetings."

The totalitarian forces are receiving Support from the dark forces of the universe

SHIO OKAWA

Do you have any hopes and goals for what Earth should achieve in 2020? How do you see Earth…

RYUHO OKAWA

"At the very least, the totalitarian forces on Earth are obviously being influenced by the dark forces of the universe. So, this is not just a battle among the people on Earth. We are thinking about how to protect this planet from behind the scenes.

"I believe this is the year to drive a huge wedge into such totalitarian hegemony."

SHIO OKAWA

And that will be the beginning of the Golden Age.

RYUHO OKAWA

"Yes. I don't know how far things will go, but either way, the situations in North Korea, South Korea, China, Hong Kong, Taiwan, and Japan are worrisome. In the ancient past, I used to live near the Tigris-Euphrates basin, closer to where Iraq and Iran are.

"These areas are also very unstable. That is why I wish to give guidance on how to manage things this year.

"In the end, we want to continue protecting this Earth that is governed by love, beauty, harmony, and peace.

"Earth should not be a place where archaic tyranny reigns or totalitarianism oppresses the people. It is unforgivable for Earth to be this way.

"As I said earlier, this is not just a battle among the people on Earth. This is a battle that involves the universe. I will not allow Ahriman*'s forces to dominate Earth any longer."

SHIO OKAWA

I see.

The wormhole point that leads to The dark universe

SHIO OKAWA

Is Ahriman from a particular star?

---

* In Zoroastrianism, Ahriman is the god of evil and the enemy of Ahura Mazda, the god of good. According to space people reading by the author, Ahriman is the evil god of the universe worshiped by malicious aliens.

RYUHO OKAWA

"It is complex to explain his star of origin. There is a world known today as the 'parallel world.' There is a force that enables us to go in and out of that world. The universe is made up of the front universe and the flip side universe. Just as Earth has heaven and hell, the universe also has heaven and hell.

"There is a wormhole point through which one can sometimes exit from the flip side universe and that is where he comes through."

SHIO OKAWA

Is there a secret to how this wormhole point forms its connection to enable access from the flip side universe?

RYUHO OKAWA

"Hmm, well, this is difficult to explain, but it tends to form in places on Earth that have their 'spiritual epicenters'."

SHIO OKAWA

So would that be somewhere above the skies of China, where the current governing system has a thought which connects with theirs?

RYUHO OKAWA

"Yes. In the previous war, that's how they got in Hitler at some point. After Hitler was defeated, they entered the Soviet Union, and now, they have moved to Communist China.

"They have moved around a lot, entering wherever they can, into both the allied and enemy forces, bringing them down one by one to create chaos to destroy the world order.

"I believe it will be a difficult year for Japan, too. Please stay true to your fundamental beliefs and persist.

"Materialism and atheism are actually acting as very powerful means to conceal these dark forces. They are great for making it seem like darkness and evil do not exist.

Technology can serve both good and evil, so that truly makes things more complicated. Yes."

SHIO OKAWA
I see.

RYUHO OKAWA
"So I'm thinking we will also need much power this year."

SHIO OKAWA
I think so, too.

RYUHO OKAWA
"It looks like China, Iran, as well as Russia and North Korea might try to connect with one another, so we must break those ties."

SHIO OKAWA
I see.

2

Questions about Planet Include

Today's UFO is shaped like
A Japanese New Year's top

SHIO OKAWA

You are shining extra brilliantly in the night sky tonight.

RYUHO OKAWA

"Yes, we are. We are shining brightly. Much brighter than the other stars."

SHIO OKAWA

Yes.

RYUHO OKAWA

"It is because we are very close to you."

SHIO OKAWA

Oh, I see.

RYUHO OKAWA

"We are pretty close. We are located about one to two kilometers away from where you are, so I guess we are just beyond Shinagawa station. In the sky above."

SHIO OKAWA

By the way, how big is the UFO you are on today?

RYUHO OKAWA

"Today's UFO resembles the shape of a spinning top used on New Year's day in Japan."

SHIO OKAWA

I see. What about the size?

RYUHO OKAWA

"The round part is about 30 m (100 ft) in diameter, and the height of the ship is about 15 m (50 ft). There is a 5-m (16-ft) deck with a shallow slope on top of the ship, and at the center of it, there is an antenna that is used for communication. It is similar to the appearance of a New Year's top."

SHIO OKAWA

Ohh. I see. How many passengers can it seat?

RYUHO OKAWA

"This one is built for 15 people."

SHIO OKAWA

OK.

Planet Include also has anniversaries

SHIO OKAWA

Sorry to ask this in the middle of a serious talk, but do you have anything like a New Year's celebration on Planet Include?

RYUHO OKAWA

"Haha."

SHIO OKAWA

[*Laughs.*] I'm just curious.

RYUHO OKAWA

"The Earth has 365 days in a year, but the length of a year differs from star to star depending on their cycle. So, it's not the same."

SHIO OKAWA

It is different.

RYUHO OKAWA

"But, almost all stars have their own celebrations with various meanings that are specific to their planet. Hmm, let me see. Well, in our case, we actually have an anniversary dedicated to me. [*Laughs.*]"

SHIO OKAWA

I see.

RYUHO OKAWA

"There are anniversaries on Planet Include, but there is no use speaking about this to you. The anniversary dedicated to me is called, 'The Anniversary of the Triumphal Return.' [*Laughs.*]"

SHIO OKAWA

Ohh.

RYUHO OKAWA

"Well, yes."

SHIO OKAWA

Does it mark your birthday or something?

RYUHO OKAWA

"Well, there was a time when I returned to the planet after achieving a certain amount of results on Earth."

SHIO OKAWA

Were they waiting for your return?

RYUHO OKAWA

"Yes, yes. There have been times when they held a welcome performance of some sort."

The situation on Earth shot in detail
From the ancient times

SHIO OKAWA

Then, do the people of Planet Include know about Earth, and are they happy about how you, Metatron, are lending your power to us?

RYUHO OKAWA

"Yes, what we are shooting is sent back and shown over there."

SHIO OKAWA

Ah.

RYUHO OKAWA

"It's a documentary."

SHIO OKAWA

So you are playing Earth's footage over there.

RYUHO OKAWA

"Yes, that's right. We were already using UFOs when I was incarnated as Metatron in ancient Mesopotamia. So, when Jesus Christ was alive, we recorded him and his activities from the sky as well. And today too. We are currently shooting this moment in a lot of detail."

SHIO OKAWA

Ohh, I see. So then, there are such exchanges happening.

RYUHO OKAWA

"Well, yes. I understand you are undergoing even tougher experiences year after year as you live as human beings."

The world of *Star Wars* is Finally about to start

RYUHO OKAWA

"It seems like this was coincidentally on TV today, but from around the time you started publishing books on spiritual interviews and readings on outer space about 10 years ago, these started influencing Japan under the surface. These are becoming common knowledge. Japan is gradually becoming less of a backward country in terms of UFO or the space information. The idea of outer space is increasingly becoming more accepted as normal.

"This year (2020) the U.S. military will form its Space Force. Japan's Self-Defense Forces also want to build their own space unit and conduct a joint manned-flight to the Moon. The purpose of this is partially to keep China in check, but they also know outer space will be the next new battle stage. It will be a fight over who gets control of the Moon.

"There are people already thinking about building a base on the Moon with capabilities of launching attacks on Earth from there, as if they are space people themselves, so you would inevitably have to set up camp on the Moon.

"So, the Space Age is about to begin during your lifetime. The world depicted in *Star Wars* is about to start. Really."

SHIO OKAWA
I see. It'll become clear.

RYUHO OKAWA
"It will begin. And when that happens, we will have a greater role to play. Right now, we must not interfere too much."

SHIO OKAWA

Will the day we meet you face to face come in our lifetime?

RYUHO OKAWA

"Right, so for that to happen, Happy Science must take on a... what do you call it... greater presence and appear more like a world religion, so that what you say is...

"If you come to have a square big enough to hold a large number of people for anniversary celebrations and is also safe for us to come down, then perhaps we can come down."

SHIO OKAWA

I see. I guess we'll have to work harder.

RYUHO OKAWA

"If you have enough land that compares to the size of Ise Grand Shrine and its precincts, we may be able to come down to you.

"We could not come down if it is a space used frequently by the public, has a lot of commercial air traffic, or is a space the Japanese Self-Defense Forces could come to. We need a certain level of security."

SHIO OKAWA
Hmm, I see.

RYUHO OKAWA
"I'm sure the HSU (Happy Science University) students are excited about 'capturing' us on film, but the chain of command for the whole group is still too shaky for this to happen. That is why I come to give my greeting only to Master Okawa for now."

We need to make religion
Prevail again in China

SHIO OKAWA

In recent years, the number of political lectures given by Master Okawa is increasing, but this year, we additionally need to include more religious and spiritual topics and also do our religious work to counter materialism and advance the Spiritual Revolution.

RYUHO OKAWA

"That's right. We cannot be on the losing side. Politics and economics join together and become one, right?

"Especially, the issue with Taiwan is closing in this year. Taiwan and also Hong Kong. We need to figure out how to deal with the situation there. Japan needs to think about what to do when working in conjunction with the United States and Europe. Right now,

Japan's decision-making is most unreliable. They need to fix this properly."

SHIO OKAWA

Under China's totalitarian regime, the truth that each human being has a soul and is the child of God with Buddha-nature is denied.

RYUHO OKAWA

"Yes. In the current state, people there are more or less being turned into human clones. If nothing changes, that is."

SHIO OKAWA

In that way, there need to be more people who know about the spiritual Truth...

RYUHO OKAWA

"Yes, yes."

SHIO OKAWA

Since politics is one of the systems for governing people, more countries need to base their politics on the spiritual Truth.

RYUHO OKAWA

"Yes. That's right."

SHIO OKAWA

Otherwise, the realm of hell on Earth will only grow.

RYUHO OKAWA

"There was a time in China when Confucianism, Taoism, and Buddhism flourished. Buddhism flourished during the Tang Dynasty as well. This time, I think they must import a new religion instead and make it popular."

SHIO OKAWA

I see.

RYUHO OKAWA

"Well, of course, Christianity will do its best too."

SHIO OKAWA

Yes.

RYUHO OKAWA

"But even in Hong Kong, there aren't just Christians living there. Buddhists and Taoists make up about several dozen percent of its population as well. We must convey our message to those people and also help India next. We must look after India until it can become a greater religious nation and join the ranks of the developed countries."

SHIO OKAWA

Yes. I understand.

3

A Message from Metatron To the People on Earth

"The final judge of Earth is El Cantare"

RYUHO OKAWA
"If you have any questions I will answer them."

SHIO OKAWA
Excuse me, could you give me a moment? The UFO is moving.

RYUHO OKAWA
"Oh, we are moving, yes."

SHIO OKAWA
I'm going to move the camera.

RYUHO OKAWA
"We are moving right now."

SHIO OKAWA

You are moving towards the upper right-hand corner.

RYUHO OKAWA

"That's right."

SHIO OKAWA

OK, the camera is set.

RYUHO OKAWA

"We are moving. Yes."

SHIO OKAWA

Now, would you give the people on Earth a message for this year?

RYUHO OKAWA

"A message?"

SHIO OKAWA

Yes, before you go.

RYUHO OKAWA

"OK. To the people of Earth, I would like you to know this: Love is indestructible. Your faith, your faith towards God is built upon love.

"Therefore, your belief in God and the activities of spreading love on this Earth should not be misunderstood as a wrong message or a sign of weakness. This is very important.

"We will not allow politics that sees human beings as tools and uses them as robots to become prevalent no matter what. That is our stance.

"In regards to the tension in Asia, a critical point will come to North Korea, Taiwan, and Hong Kong this year.

"As for Iran, there will be a battle to decide whether to patch up differences or to enforce a reformation. But I believe the final judge on matters relating to Earth is El Cantare."

SHIO OKAWA
Yes. That's right.

RYUHO OKAWA
"We have our opinions, but El Cantare has the final authority. El Cantare is the one who is responsible for Earth, so we too will make our final decisions based on El Cantare's thoughts.

"It is possible to intervene from outer space. But Earth has not reached a stage where a full-scale intervention is possible. So, it is our job to send messages to the leaders on Earth to show them the way."

SHIO OKAWA

I see.

"Taiwan and Hong Kong can potentially Change the destiny of Earth"

SHIO OKAWA

Mr. Metatron, given that you communicate with Master Okawa in this way...

RYUHO OKAWA

"Yes, yes. I do."

SHIO OKAWA

Do you happen to communicate with El Cantare in any other way?

RYUHO OKAWA

"Hmm?"

SHIO OKAWA

Do you communicate with El Cantare spiritually on, say, a daily basis?

RYUHO OKAWA

"Every day, huh?"

SHIO OKAWA

Maybe you don't talk every day.

RYUHO OKAWA

"Well, maybe not every day. When he has a large task at hand, I most certainly approach and cooperate, but it's not all the time. The work is divided and shared.

"However, there is still last year's work in Taiwan left to be done this year. Taiwan and Hong Kong can potentially change the destiny of Earth."

SHIO OKAWA

Ah... So they are big factors.

RYUHO OKAWA

"I feel I am the one to push forward in these areas. We just have to do it.

"A savior must not waver in this conviction, so I will do my best here. The importance of speaking out about what is right cannot be overstressed. That is why I want to change Japan's spineless, jellyfish-like qualities."

SHIO OKAWA

Yes. Thank you so much for that.

There is a possibility for various changes to Occur around the world this year

SHIO OKAWA

This year Master Okawa is planning to go on a missionary tour to the U.K. and the United States.

RYUHO OKAWA

"Right, the U.K. and America. But something might happen and require him to travel to other countries too... Well, there is a possibility for that."

SHIO OKAWA

Oh, really. For example?

RYUHO OKAWA

"Hahaha."

SHIO OKAWA

[*Laughs*.] Is it still undecided?

RYUHO OKAWA

"For example, South Korea could be one. He may have to go there."

SHIO OKAWA

Ah…

RYUHO OKAWA

"He may also need to go to Taiwan. There could also be a chance to go to Thailand."

SHIO OKAWA

Wow. That must mean that it is very likely for many changes to happen on Earth.

RYUHO OKAWA

"We must look out for the Asian regions, but we cannot say that Iran *isn't* on the list."

SHIO OKAWA

Ohh.

RYUHO OKAWA

"If the possibility of war in Iran becomes real, they may even reach out to you."

SHIO OKAWA

What should ideally happen is not war, but for the U.S. and Iran to come to a point where they can talk.

RYUHO OKAWA

"So, an opportunity to meet the Iranian President or President of the United States might arise."

SHIO OKAWA

I see.

The awareness of being a savior changes
With the size and achievements of the task

RYUHO OKAWA

"But your organization as a whole is still not strong enough. Your political party is especially weak in terms of elections. They don't have much power.

"We in outer space want to do something about this, but just as Jesus Christ couldn't be as influential in politics while he was alive, things are not so easy. It is difficult to triumph over traditional powers. It's not like someone will vote for your party just because Happy Science cured their illness. Nor will they vote because its prophecy came true. Votes are ultimately determined by people with this-worldly values pursuing this-worldly interests.

"But the awareness of a savior changes depending on the scale of the work he does or the results he achieves. He has not reached the final level yet. He has indeed attained the Seventh Sense, which is the ability to communicate with space people. But he needs to attain the awareness of being a messiah on a cosmic level."

SHIO OKAWA

I see. So, you are saying that Master Okawa's work has cosmic significance.

RYUHO OKAWA

"Yes. But because the worldly fighting powers of Happy Science are so weak, he is unable to reach the next level. Well, I am actually holding back from saying much more because my earnest comments can be too harsh."

SHIO OKAWA

I'm sorry.

RYUHO OKAWA

"My message must be adjusted by the guiding spirits of Earth. Otherwise, it will be too severe."

SHIO OKAWA

I understand.

RYUHO OKAWA

"Well, I just want to say, I'll be here supporting you this year too. Yaidron will come to give his greetings on another day."

SHIO OKAWA

Yes. We are truly grateful for you every day. Thank you.

RYUHO OKAWA

"Yes. I'm here on New Year's."

SHIO OKAWA

Yes. Happy New Year. Please give us your guidance and strength this year, too.

RYUHO OKAWA

"Yes, I will."

SHIO OKAWA

Thank you very much.

Chapter 2

R.A. Goal's Message
– UFO Reading 42 –

*Originally recorded in Japanese on January 3, 2020
at Special Lecture Hall, Happy Science, Japan
and later translated into English*

R.A. Goal

A space being from Planet Andalucia Beta in Ursa Minor. One of the commanders of the space defense force. A certified messiah.

Interviewers from Happy Science[*]

Shio Okawa
Aide to Master & CEO

*The opinions of the space being do not necessarily reflect those of
Happy Science Group.*

---

[*] Her professional title represents her position at the time of the interview.

1

A "Bright Light" That Appeared At a Low Position In the Sky Above Tokyo

RYUHO OKAWA

It's in the direction towards the southwest. At an extremely low position in the sky above Minato Ward in Tokyo, there is a very powerful light. It's rare to see one so low and powerful. There was nothing in this part of the sky yesterday.

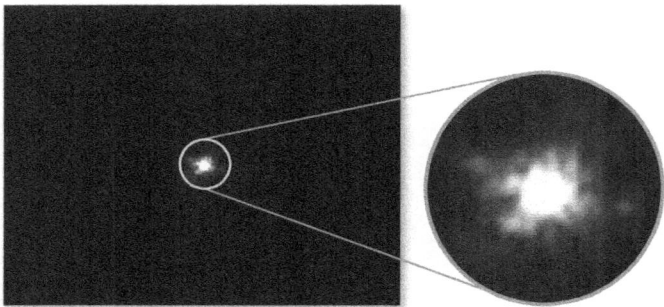

R.A. Goal's UFO captured in this recording session
Spotted by Ryuho Okawa / Video taken by Shio Okawa
January 3, 2020 at 6:03 pm in Tokyo (right: enlarged image)

We can see some other smaller flying objects moving in the sky, but they are small. They are much smaller, and this is the only one flying so low and emitting such a strong light. [*About 5 seconds of silence.*] Are you able to capture it?

SHIO OKAWA

I had it just a moment ago. Please hold on…

RYUHO OKAWA

It might move and hide behind the trees. We could capture it better if it flew a little higher. I wonder if they can.

SHIO OKAWA

It's going towards the trees…

RYUHO OKAWA

It looks like the trees might get in the way.

SHIO OKAWA

Oh, I got it.

RYUHO OKAWA

Is it on camera?

SHIO OKAWA

Yes.

RYUHO OKAWA

Alright, shall I have a quick talk while it's on camera?

SHIO OKAWA

I'm going to zoom in a little... [*About 10 seconds of silence.*] OK.

RYUHO OKAWA

OK. It is at an extremely low position in the sky above Minato Ward.

It is almost 6 pm right now. Since it is January, it is already very dark outside.

Today is January 3. A little before 6 pm on the 3rd.

There is a large object emitting a very strong light from an extremely low position in the sky. It's large. To describe just how large it is, it is impossible for a star to be so big.

There are many other small stars scattered across the sky, but among them are moving ones so some of them might be UFOs. There is a particularly strong will coming from this low one...

SHIO OKAWA
It's oddly bright.

RYUHO OKAWA
Yes. I'd like to start talking to it. We might not have much time to capture it. There is a strong chance it will hide behind the trees.

OK, to the one who is emitting a strong light from an extremely low position in the sky. Who might I be speaking to, please?

[*About 10 seconds of silence.*]

2

Predicting a Very Tough Start to 2020

"Some unbelievable things Will happen to China"

* All texts in bold and quotation marks are the words directly spoken by the space being in a spiritual reading with Ryuho Okawa.

RYUHO OKAWA

He is a little different from who I was expecting. He says **"I am R.L. Gool."**

SHIO OKAWA

Oh.

RYUHO OKAWA

Have we come across anyone like this?

198

SHIO OKAWA

R.A... I think so.

RYUHO OKAWA

He is calling himself "R.A. Gool." He is saying, "I'm R.A. Gool."

SHIO OKAWA

One moment, please. [*About 25 seconds of silence.*] (Translator's note: *Looking through the records of past UFO readings.*) Hmm. I'm pretty sure there was someone named "R.A. Gool" before.*

RYUHO OKAWA

Oh, I see. It looks like it will soon disappear from our sight...

---

* When the author recorded spiritual readings on UFOs on September 16 and October 21, 2018, R.A. Goal appeared. He is also called "Mr. R" and "Master R". See Ryuho Okawa, *UFOs Caught on Camera!: A Spiritual Investigation on Videos and Photos of the Luminous Objects Visiting Earth* (Tokyo: HS Press, 2018).

SHIO OKAWA

In that case, please ask him for a message.

RYUHO OKAWA

OK. Please give us your message. What kind of message would you like to... Did you come here to tell us something? Please send us a message. [*About 5 seconds of silence.*]

He is saying, "**The Chinese military will attack imminently.**"

SHIO OKAWA

Who will they attack?

RYUHO OKAWA

He says, "**China will initiate the attacks in a way that the world will recognize as a threat. Hong Kong, Taiwan, or both will be targeted, but it could go as far as the Senkaku Islands. The target will be that general area. This is to immobilize the U.S. military. At the same** time, North Korea will show their menacing behavior to the other countries as well. You may have an extremely tough time right from the very beginning of the year."

SHIO OKAWA

I see.

RYUHO OKAWA

"China's intention is to make the world kneel before them no matter what. Their intentions and desires to intimidate and make international society kneel before them will come to light very clearly this year.

"Japan will soon... Although the people are now enjoying a peaceful New Year's holiday, there is a strong possibility for another era of evacuation sirens to return.

"It may be uncertain whether the Olympics can even be held. You have to be ready because this year may not be so easy to get through."

SHIO OKAWA

I see. Have you come today to warn us of the prospects of this year?

RYUHO OKAWA

"And some of us, here in space, threat... even though we are in space, we plan to make a threatening attack. We will take a threatening action against China. I think some unbelievable occurrences will take place."

SHIO OKAWA

I see.

RYUHO OKAWA

"Yes. Since they don't believe in God, we will cause things that appear to be natural disasters but could also be seen as God's will. Please keep a close watch."

SHIO OKAWA
OK.

All that Prime Minister Abe
Neglected to do will cause a bad consequence

RYUHO OKAWA

"Please lead the Japanese public opinion in the rightful direction."

SHIO OKAWA

Yes.

RYUHO OKAWA

"Our conclusion is that Japan must not invite Xi Jinping as a state guest this spring. They (China) will protest and even use force to make it happen. That's their nature."

SHIO OKAWA

Yes.

RYUHO OKAWA

"We need to lead the world in the right direction.

"Mr. Trump needs to focus his attention on the crises in Asia, not on the crises in the Persian Gulf.

"China is planning something extremely dangerous."

SHIO OKAWA
I see.

RYUHO OKAWA
"Right now, they are constructing many missile bases on the southern coast of China. There will be many Chinese government vessels that come to the Senkaku Islands. They are doing this so that they could prepare to initiate missile strikes simultaneously.

"Soon they are going to take an old-fashioned approach where they threaten and force their opponent into submission, much like during the Mongol invasions of Japan."

SHIO OKAWA
Yes.

RYUHO OKAWA
"There is an airplane flying above me, but such a peaceful time may not last very long. Unless you prepare now, you may run out of time."

SHIO OKAWA
I see.

RYUHO OKAWA
"Japan is probably more concerned about the Cherry Blossom Viewing Party or whether the Olympics can take place, or whether the economy will improve after that. But there are things to be done more urgently that were not accomplished. There are things Prime Minister Abe should have

done without wasting time. The constitution wasn't amended, a peace treaty with Russia was never agreed upon, and the issue with Iran was not dealt with. And nothing was said regarding Hong Kong. Nothing was done to help Taiwan either. All these things that he neglected to do will bring about a bad consequence at once."

SHIO OKAWA
I see.

RYUHO OKAWA
"Yes, so I believe a crisis will occur relatively soon."

SHIO OKAWA
I understand.

We in space will take countermeasures
Against some of China's actions

RYUHO OKAWA

"You all on Earth probably have close to no power to counter events of this scale, so we will assist you in some way from outer space. Please take note of those occurrences carefully."

SHIO OKAWA

OK.

RYUHO OKAWA

"We also embody a part of what has been called God from ancient times. Yes."

SHIO OKAWA

Are you on the same side as Mr. Metatron?

RYUHO OKAWA

"Ah yes, we do keep in contact. However, Metatron and his team won't go as far as to attack."

SHIO OKAWA

I see.

RYUHO OKAWA

"But we are preparing to intervene."

SHIO OKAWA

Mr. R.A. Gool. Are you the same as R.A. 1…

RYUHO OKAWA

"R.A. Goal."

SHIO OKAWA

R.A. Goal. OK. And by the way…

RYUHO OKAWA

"Well, it's actually a hidden name. I can't reveal my real name, but I am one of the commanders of the defense force in space."

SHIO OKAWA

OK.

The UFO is starting to get covered up by the trees... I'm sorry.

RYUHO OKAWA

"Ah, perhaps you won't be able to see me soon."

SHIO OKAWA

And lastly, the UFO we see today, it's either very big or very near to us. The shape, or rather, the light is impressive.

RYUHO OKAWA

"The total length of this UFO is about 70 m
(230 ft)."

SHIO OKAWA

About 70 m.

RYUHO OKAWA

"That's right. It's a larger model. Well, I guess
it's between a medium and a large model. It's
actually an offensive UFO."

SHIO OKAWA

Oh, I see.

RYUHO OKAWA

"Yes. This ship carries several smaller vessels,
which are about a few meters in length, and
can take off from here. We are considering
that, if China decides to use their missile bases
on the southern coast to attack Taiwan, Hong

Kong, or the Senkaku Islands or Okinawa of Japan, we will destroy those bases."

SHIO OKAWA

I see.

RYUHO OKAWA

"Yes. We are currently on guard. These are the things I wanted to convey to you today."

SHIO OKAWA

I understand. Thank you very much for the valuable guidelines.

RYUHO OKAWA

Thank you very much. [*Claps hands once.*] It wasn't Yaidron.

Note: The battleship UFO of R.A. Goal disappeared 1.5 hours after the recording.

Chapter 3

Spiritual Messages from the Guardian Spirit of President Moon Jae-in and Yaidron

*Originally recorded in Japanese on February 5, 2020
at Special Lecture Hall, Happy Science, Japan
and later translated into English*

Moon Jae-in (1953 - Present)

The President of the Republic of Korea. Graduated from Kyung Hee University. As a student, Moon was imprisoned for participating in a democratization movement against the Park Chung-hee administration. After passing the bar exam in 1980 and becoming a lawyer, he opened a law office with Roh Moo-hyun, who later became president of South Korea. During the Roh administration, Moon served in positions such as the presidential chief of staff. Subsequently, after holding positions such as the leader of the Democratic Party of Korea, he took office as the 19th president of South Korea in May 2017.

Yaidron

A space being from Planet Elder in the Magellanic Clouds. He is a powerful being with higher-dimensional powers in the Earth Spirit World and is a god of justice. Yaidron is currently protecting Master Ryuho Okawa, the human incarnation of El Cantare, God of the Earth. He has been involved with the rise and fall of civilizations, wars, and major disasters on Earth.

Interviewers from Happy Science[*]

Sakurako Jinmu
Managing Director
Chief Secretary, First Secretarial Division
Religious Affairs Headquarters

Shio Okawa
Aide to Master & CEO

No statements made by the guardian spirit of Mr. Moon Jae-in in this book reflect statements actually made by Mr. Moon Jae-in himself.

The opinions of the spirits do not necessarily reflect those of Happy Science Group. For the mechanism behind spiritual messages, see the end section.

---

[*] Interviewers are listed in the order that they appear in the transcript.
Their professional titles represent their positions at the time of the interview.

1

Moon Jae-in's Guardian Spirit Suddenly Appears

He threatens that everyone will die soon

[*Editor's Note: Playing in the background is a recording of the author's original song "Let's Go With Self-Help" — the supporter's anthem for Angel Shoja.*]

PRESIDENT MOON'S GUARDIAN SPIRIT
Hah… Hah… [*Breathes heavily.*]

JINMU
Hello.

MOON'S G.S.
Hah…

JINMU
Who is this?

MOON'S G.S.

Hah… [*About 5 seconds of silence.*] Hah… Hah.
[*About 5 seconds of silence.*] Hah…

SHIO OKAWA

Are you someone who likes self-help? Or are you
someone who doesn't?

MOON'S G.S.

[*About 10 seconds of silence.*] Hah.

SHIO OKAWA

Are you suffering? Are you Japanese?

JINMU

Are you someone who likes Japan? Are you a
human?

MOON'S G.S.

[*About 5 seconds of silence.*] Hah… Hah.

SHIO OKAWA

"Let's Go With Self-Help" is a song about the opposite of self-centeredness.

MOON'S G.S.

Hah. Hah.

SHIO OKAWA

Do you want to keep listening to it?

MOON'S G.S.

Hah. Hah. [*About 5 seconds of silence.*] Hah... [*About 10 seconds of silence.*] Hah... S... Soon... Soon...

SHIO OKAWA

Yes?

MOON'S G.S.

Soon...

SHIO OKAWA
What?

MOON'S G.S.
Soon…

JINMU
"Soon"?

MOON'S G.S.
Die.

SHIO OKAWA
Who?

MOON'S G.S.
Everyone.

JINMU
Everyone?

MOON'S G.S.
You'll all die.

JINMU
What country are you from?

MOON'S G.S.
Huh?

SHIO OKAWA
Is it Korea?

JINMU
Are you from Korea?

MOON'S G.S.
I live in the Land of God.

SHIO OKAWA
And where is the "Land of God?"

MOON'S G.S.

Hmm? Across the sea.

SHIO OKAWA

China? Oh, you're being attacked by the coronavirus. Are you Mr. Xi Jinping's guardian spirit?

JINMU

Is it Xi Jinping?

SHIO OKAWA

Aren't you Mr. Xi Jinping? Are you being attacked by the coronavirus?

JINMU

Are you in trouble?

SHIO OKAWA

…Because you can't drive the virus out?

JINMU

Is it Mr. Xi Jinping? Is it Xi Jinping?

MOON'S G.S.

[*In an angry manner.*] I'm Moon Jae-in!

Words of hatred and anger towards Japan

SHIO OKAWA

Why has Moon Jae-in come to us?

MOON'S G.S.

You saw the film, didn't you?

SHIO OKAWA

A South Korean film? [*Editor's Note: They were watching the South Korean film* Fengshui *just before this spiritual interview.*]

MOON'S G.S.

Yeah. You don't understand that masterpiece, so you deserve to die!

SHIO OKAWA

You should have told us about your identity earlier. You're a president after all.

MOON'S G.S.

I'm telling you, I'm a king of the royal family.

JINMU

Are you related to someone in the film?

SHIO OKAWA

Did you come because you are in tune with the movie?

MOON'S G.S.

Yeah. I'm trying to take back what Japan took from us! Tsk.

SHIO OKAWA
Is South Korea in that much trouble right now?

MOON'S G.S.
Are you stupid? Tsk. Tsk.

SHIO OKAWA
What's wrong? What's making you suffer?

MOON'S G.S.
What?

SHIO OKAWA
Is there something that's making you suffer?

MOON'S G.S.
Of course, I'm suffering.

SHIO OKAWA
The coronavirus hasn't spread to South Korea
that much yet.

MOON'S G.S.

What are you talking about? I mean we need to carry on the line of royal succession up to the second generation.

SHIO OKAWA

We've been told that the North Korean succession will end during the third generation.

MOON'S G.S.

Then we just have to look for a new land.

SHIO OKAWA

That's not possible because your country isn't so big. Did you come to us because we were watching the film?

MOON'S G.S.

It was born on Paektu Mountain and has continued to the third generation.

SHIO OKAWA

Do you want to go to North Korea?

MOON'S G.S.

That's my fatherland.

SHIO OKAWA

And do you want to unify Korea?

MOON'S G.S.

Of course, I do.

SHIO OKAWA

But the Prosecution Office is charging and indicting the people around you. Do you think you can remain in government?

MOON'S G.S.

[*About 5 seconds of silence.*] Yeah. Abe will be arrested first.

SHIO OKAWA

So, you'll eventually be arrested as well?

MOON'S G.S.

I'm impermeable, but Abe will soon be arrested.

SHIO OKAWA

Why are you suffering so much?

MOON'S G.S.

The Tokyo Olympics will be crushed.

He won't even try to understand causal Retribution and self-responsibility

SHIO OKAWA

We were watching the film *Fengshui* and they blamed almost everything on the land, the environment, and their ancestors.

MOON'S G.S.

That's right.

SHIO OKAWA

Is that the right attitude to have?

MOON'S G.S.

It's all because of that poor land. We get bullied a lot by China, Japan, and Russia.

JINMU

How did you feel listening to the song "Let's Go With Self-Help"?

MOON'S G.S.

Like I care.

SHIO OKAWA

You basically don't learn about self-help, is that right? Do you understand what "causal retribution" is?

MOON'S G.S.

Go and tell some other country.

JINMU

Is there anything else you would like to say?

SHIO OKAWA

If not, we needn't continue.

MOON'S G.S.

I hate Takamori Saigo* the most, I tell you. I know him.

SHIO OKAWA

Why?

MOON'S G.S.

Who advocated that Japan should conquer Korea?

---

* Takamori Saigo [1828-1877] a Japanese military official, politician, and one of the key figures of the Meiji Restoration.

SHIO OKAWA

Ah…

MOON'S G.S.

His grave— I really want to dig up his grave. It doesn't have a head.

JINMU

OK, can we finish this, please?

MOON'S G.S.

According to Feng shui, Kagoshima is a land of bad luck.

JINMU

No, forget about Feng shui. Geopolitically, South Korea is an important place for Japan.

MOON'S G.S.

That's why you've wanted to invade our country since the Meiji Restoration. It's a huge problem.

SHIO OKAWA

We don't have anything we particularly want to talk to you about right now.

MOON'S G.S.

What are you saying? Reflect on your evils. What are you taking exams* for? Go and reflect!

SHIO OKAWA

Yeah, Mr. Moon Jae-in always thinks, "Other people are to blame for everything."

MOON'S G.S.

Isn't that right? We live bearing the curse of having been born in this land.

SHIO OKAWA

A former Japanese foreign correspondent based in South Korea wrote an article on the Internet, and

---

* Happy Science staff members were taking a staff-only qualification exam on the same morning (February 5, 2020).

said that President Moon is "the spitting image of Roh Moo-hyun, meaning, I can see Moon Jae-in's last days."

MOON'S G.S.
Then, I'll use "electric shock."

SHIO OKAWA
So, you know about "electric shock."

MOON'S G.S.
Burn him.

SHIO OKAWA
How do you know about that? Have you ever received it?

MOON'S G.S.
It's being talked about a lot here. You've been doing evil things to China.

SHIO OKAWA

No, we haven't.

MOON'S G.S.

You sure have.

SHIO OKAWA

No, that was the "causal retribution" that China brought upon itself.

MOON'S G.S.

As punishment, you will get infected by the coronavirus and die.

SHIO OKAWA

I was coughing just during lunchtime. Was that your curse?

MOON'S G.S.

I'll grant you your final wish. Get on a pleasure boat and get out of Japan.

SHIO OKAWA

What? You'll grant my final wish?

MOON'S G.S.

Yeah. Then, everyone will get infected by the coronavirus you have and die.

SHIO OKAWA

Then, I wish for the Happy Science teachings to spread in South Korea.

MOON'S G.S.

No, that's not allowed. Because we're exterminating it now.

SHIO OKAWA

"Causal retribution." "Self-responsibility."

MOON'S G.S.

We're disinfecting the country right now, so those sorts of evil teachings can't enter.

JINMU

Then, please leave. We have no business with you.

MOON'S G.S.

You shut up and find your head.*

JINMU

That doesn't matter because the body will eventually turn into soil.

---

* According to spiritual readings by the author, Jinmu was likely born as Takamori Saigo in a past life.

2

Yaidron's Predictions of the Near Future In Asia and the World

Yaidron's electric shock

SHIO OKAWA

Then, we'll give you a taste of the electric shock. You want it, don't you? You want to experience it, right?

MOON'S G.S.

Don't you want to transform into a woman?

SHIO OKAWA

Shall we call on Mr. Yaidron?

MOON'S G.S.

See if I care!

SHIO OKAWA

Oh, Mr. Yaidron.

JINMU

It's an other-dimensional strike.

SHIO OKAWA

Oh, Mr. Yaidron.

JINMU

Mr. Yaidron, please cast your electric shock.

[*About 15 seconds of silence.*]

YAIDRON

Haa… [*Exhales.*] This is Yaidron.

SHIO OKAWA

That's cool.

JINMU

Thank you very much.

China's economic downturn is imminent, And South Korea will be isolated

YAIDRON

South Korea is in trouble right now.

SHIO OKAWA

Why is that?

YAIDRON

China is now in total lockdown. A downturn in China's economy is imminent.

SHIO OKAWA

Oh!

YAIDRON

Xi Jinping's position is already at risk. His policy of balancing other powers is becoming ineffective. South Korea will be isolated.

SHIO OKAWA

You mean because they live off China's backing.

YAIDRON

South Korea was getting ready to cooperate with China to lift the economic blockade on North Korea.

SHIO OKAWA

I see.

YAIDRON

They weren't expecting China to lockdown like that. So now, they're in trouble. South Korea's economy will definitely get worse, and they're also quarreling with Japan. So, they can't ask for aid from Japan.

SHIO OKAWA

Ah, right. I see.

YAIDRON

Yes. So, South Korea will self-destruct if they keep going as they are. They will collapse before Japan does. If China is headed towards a recession, South Korea will collapse first.

SHIO OKAWA

Before Japan?

YAIDRON

Yes. And the U.S. hates Moon Jae-in at the moment, so they don't intend to give aid.

SHIO OKAWA

But since South Korea needs to change, it can't be helped.

YAIDRON

They're simultaneously encircling China and trying to destroy Moon Jae-in.

SHIO OKAWA

The U.S.?

YAIDRON

Yes. They intend to destroy the Moon Jae-in administration. To destroy it and North. . . Well, one of their strategies is not to let anyone support North Korea. They're not just doing it to Iran. They're doing good work too.

SHIO OKAWA

I see.

YAIDRON

Yes. They think they need to cut off any powers that are supporting North Korea.

The dire situation with
The Abe administration

YAIDRON

Mr. Abe is also nearing his end. This is unmistakable.

The U.S. is now considering who should lead the Japanese government next. They're thinking about who will make things work best. Abe's time is up when they come to a decision.

In the U.S., the Democratic Party will face a momentous defeat. The party is in such chaos that they can't even decide on a presidential candidate. They obviously cannot win, no matter who runs.

So, Trump is rapidly regaining his power. And now it won't just be Iran: he'll finally begin his strike on North Korea and China. Things will start intensifying from springtime.

SHIO OKAWA

Trump is not Yahweh[*], is he?

YAIDRON

I think he's saying, "I have greater power than the so-called almighty God of that tiny country."

SHIO OKAWA

I see.

YAIDRON

Well, it's understandable.

SHIO OKAWA

Yes, considering he's the President of the United States.

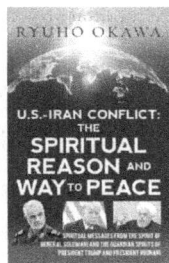

---

[*] See Ryuho Okawa, *U.S.-Iran Conflict: the Spiritual Reason and Way to Peace -Spiritual Messages from the Spirit of General Soleimani and the Guardian Spirits of President Trump and President Rouhani-* (Tokyo: HS Press, 2020).

YAIDRON

He's more than capable of destroying an entire country, so he definitely has as much power as Yahweh. The U.S. is capable of fighting against the United Nations, and even the whole world.

So, North Korea... You people might only be thinking about the virus in China, but things collapse from the weakest places.

SHIO OKAWA

At times like this.

YAIDRON

Yes. So right now, South Korea is about to collapse. Their economic support for North Korea will break down, and China's economic support for North and South Korea will also break down. The floodgates will close in one swift move.

SHIO OKAWA

Right.

YAIDRON

Moon Jae-in is fighting against prosecution, but that will soon collapse. The administration is on the brink of collapse. It's the same with Japan's Prosecutor's Office and the Abe administration. It's a race to see who will fall first.

Japan's power structure is about to change, with the turning point being Xi Jinping's big moment. There is a movement against letting him see Japan's cherry blossoms.

SHIO OKAWA

Right, thank you.

The Golden Age and the year
The "Great Wall" will be destroyed

YAIDRON

South Korea is actually losing quite a bit of strength. And the people are beginning to say,

"We're suffering because the government started quarreling with Japan." North Korea is no good, and China is completely undependable. Many people are saying, "We can't survive unless we get along with Japan." Taiwan and Hong Kong are looking to Japan. The age of the Look East Policy is about to begin again.

China's fragility will be uncovered in various ways. They don't even have a proper medical system, and with information, all they ever do is control it. They don't communicate good information; they don't even have information that will help people. They only ever react after the incident takes place. And now they're trying hard to create a bulwark to keep the virus out of Beijing. Anyway, Beijing is nearing its end.

So, I want to say, "Don't underestimate this year: the Golden Age." The Golden Age is the year the "Great Wall" collapses.

On the other hand, I don't care what happens with the Olympics.

SHIO OKAWA

We, the Earthlings, have to work harder.

YAIDRON

If the — what is it, coronavirus? If that spreads more, the Olympics will be out of the question. If people gather in Japan, the virus will spread from the Olympic Village throughout the world; all of the places where many people gather, from indoor stadiums to everywhere else will be affected. After all, people think it's dangerous to gather.

So, this is putting a huge pressure on the government right now. It's not just about Moon Jae-in, it's about Xi Jinping and how much this coronavirus scare will spread. It's severer than the SARS outbreak, and people are slowly starting to realize the cause behind it. They are now realizing that this is one possible way (to stop evil).

The South Korean government
Will be overthrown

YAIDRON

You must understand that Moon Jae-in just came in screaming. South Korea no longer has a future. Neither does North Korea. North Korea wanted to launch their long-range missiles, but they're now occupied with the virus outbreak. If they launch missiles at a time like this, people will think that the leaders have gone crazy, so they can't do it.

Well, there will be major changes. Hong Kong is also moving towards independence.

SHIO OKAWA

I see.

YAIDRON

Of course, Taiwan has also declared that they are not part of the People's Republic of China. I think something interesting is about to happen.

SHIO OKAWA

Right.

YAIDRON

And there will probably be political upheaval in South Korea: the government will be overthrown.

Not only is the Prosecutor's Office changing its views, but the public opinion is also changing rapidly. People are starting to think that it was a mistake to justify the administration based on Japan-hate and anti-Japanese sentiments alone.

They'll start to think of Moon Jae-in as a Fascist tyrant; a man who cooperated with evil North Korea and used the anti-Japan sentiment to make the country stronger, a traitor.

Don't underestimate El Cantare

YAIDRON

So, I don't think anyone will be concerning themselves with the Olympics this year, maybe. But I think many things will turn out better that way.

SHIO OKAWA

Thank you.

YAIDRON

We have so much we want to say. We're all trying hard not to say everything.

SHIO OKAWA

We understand that you have to do some of these things without telling us.

YAIDRON

Yes, there are things we have to do without telling you.

SHIO OKAWA

We just feel really ashamed of ourselves.

YAIDRON

We're warning people not to underestimate El Cantare.

SHIO OKAWA

Right.

YAIDRON

Yes. The people around the world underestimate Him, and so do the people of Japan. So, we're saying, don't underestimate Him.

SHIO OKAWA

Thank you.

YAIDRON

OK.

JINMU

Thank you.

RYUHO OKAWA

[*Claps twice.*]

Afterword

The majority of Japanese and Chinese readers might say, "Messages from outer space? No way," especially since the afterworld and existence of spirits are challenging enough to believe.

In this book, I have revealed that there are entities with clear intentions that are getting involved with Earth. I've relayed the warning delivered by a space being with the hidden name, "R.A. Goal."

I have no interest in coercing people to believe the thoughts introduced here. However, given my past records, I don't doubt that I can identify the reasons behind large-scale disasters.

It is likely that *Onmyojis* (Yin-Yang Masters) from the Middle Ages or the prophets of the ancient times deciphered some form of heavenly will. There is a need for this in the current times. Not all decisions are made solely by the humans who live on Earth.

Ryuho Okawa
Master & CEO of Happy Science Group
Feb. 11, 2020

ABOUT THE AUTHOR

RYUHO OKAWA was born on July 7th 1956, in Tokushima prefecture, Japan. After graduating from the University of Tokyo with a law degree, he joined a Tokyo-based trading house. While working at its New York headquarters, he studied international finance at the Graduate Center of the City University of New York. In 1981, he attained Great Enlightenment and became aware that he is El Cantare with a mission to bring salvation to all of humankind. In 1986 he established Happy Science. It now has members in over 100 countries across the world, with more than 700 local branches and temples as well as 10,000 missionary houses around the world. The total number of lectures has exceeded 3,000 (of which more than 150 are in English) and over 2,600 books (of which more than 500 are Spiritual Interview Series) have been published, many of which are translated into 31 languages. Many of the books, including *The Laws of the Sun* have become best sellers or million sellers. To date, Happy Science has produced 20 movies. The original story and original concept were given by the Executive Producer Ryuho Okawa. Recent movie titles are *The Real Exorcist* (live-action movie to be released in May 2020), *Kiseki to no Deai - Kokoro ni Yorisou 3 -* (lit. "Encounters with Miracles - Heart to Heart 3 -," documentary scheduled to be released in Aug. 2020), and *Twiceborn* (live-action movie to be released in Fall of 2020). He has also composed the lyrics and music of over 100 songs, such as theme songs and featured songs of movies. Moreover, he is the Founder of Happy Science University and Happy Science Academy (Junior and Senior High School), Founder and President of the Happiness Realization Party, Founder and Honorary Headmaster of Happy Science Institute of Government and Management, Founder of IRH Press Co., Ltd., and the Chairperson of New Star Production Co., Ltd. and ARI Production Co., Ltd.

WHAT IS EL CANTARE?

El Cantare means "the Light of the Earth," and is the Supreme God of the Earth who has been guiding humankind since the beginning of Genesis. He is whom Jesus called Father. Different parts of El Cantare's core consciousness have descended to Earth in the past, once as Alpha and another as Elohim. His branch spirits, such as Shakyamuni Buddha and Hermes, have descended to Earth many times and helped to flourish many civilizations. To unite various religions and to integrate various fields of study in order to build a new civilization on Earth, a part of the core consciousness has descended to Earth as Master Ryuho Okawa.

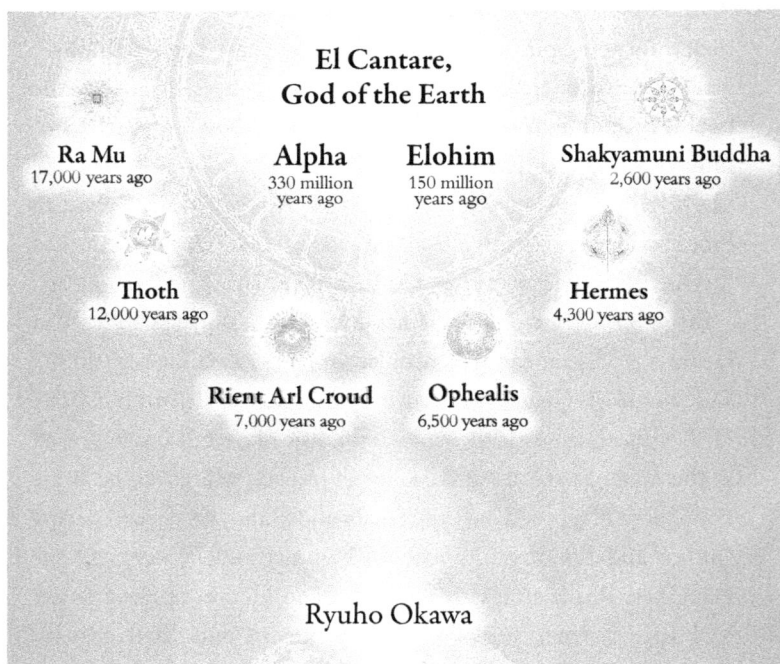

**El Cantare,
God of the Earth**

Ra Mu	**Alpha**	**Elohim**	**Shakyamuni Buddha**
17,000 years ago	330 million years ago	150 million years ago	2,600 years ago

Thoth
12,000 years ago

Hermes
4,300 years ago

Rient Arl Croud
7,000 years ago

Ophealis
6,500 years ago

Ryuho Okawa

Alpha Alpha is a part of the core consciousness of El Cantare that descended to Earth about 330 million years ago. Alpha preached Earth's Truths to harmonize and unify Earth-born humans and space people who came from other planets.

Elohim Elohim is the name of El Cantare's core consciousness that lived on Earth 150 million years ago. He taught teachings of wisdom, mainly on the differences of light and darkness, good and evil.

Shakyamuni Buddha Gautama Siddhartha was born as a prince into the Shakya Clan in India around 2,600 years ago. When he was 29 years old, he renounced the world and sought enlightenment. He later attained Great Enlightenment and founded Buddhism.

Hermes In the Greek mythology, Hermes is thought of as one of the 12 Olympian gods, but the spiritual Truth is that he taught the teachings of love and progress around 4,300 years ago that became the origin of the current Western civilization. He is a hero that truly existed.

Ophealis Ophealis was born in Greece around 6,500 years ago and was the leader who took an expedition to as far as Egypt. He is the God of miracles, prosperity, and arts, and is known as Osiris in the Egyptian mythology.

Rient Arl Croud Rient Arl Croud was born as a king of the ancient Incan Empire around 7,000 years ago and taught about the mysteries of the mind. In the heavenly world, he is responsible for the interactions that take place between various planets.

Thoth Thoth was an almighty leader who built the golden age of the Atlantic civilization around 12,000 years ago. In the Egyptian mythology, he is known as God Thoth.

Ra Mu Ra Mu was a leader who built the golden age of the civilization of Mu around 17,000 years ago. As a religious leader and a politician, he ruled by uniting religion and politics.

WHAT IS A SPIRITUAL MESSAGE?

We are all spiritual beings living on this earth. The following is the mechanism behind Master Ryuho Okawa's spiritual messages.

1 You are a spirit

People are born into this world to gain wisdom through various experiences and return to the other world when their lives end. We are all spirits and repeat this cycle in order to refine our souls.

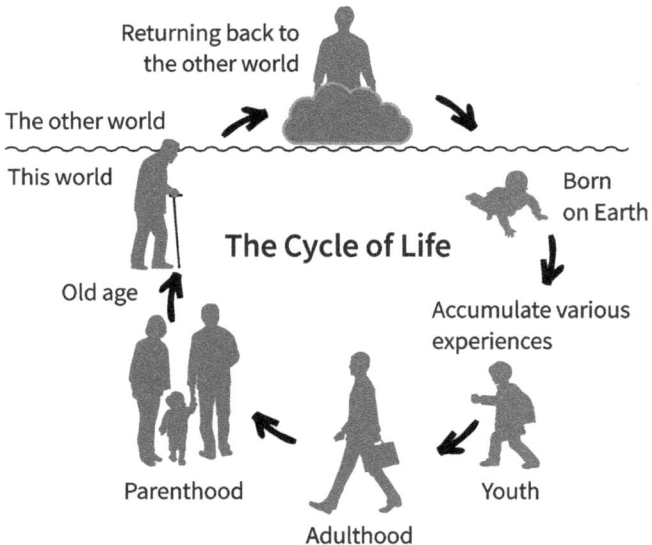

Returning back to
the other world

The other world

This world

Born
on Earth

The Cycle of Life

Old age

Accumulate various
experiences

Parenthood

Youth

Adulthood

2 You have a guardian spirit

Guardian spirits are those who protect the people who are living on this earth. Each of us has a guardian spirit that watches over us and guides us from the other world. They were us in our past life, and are identical in how we think.

The other world

Guardian Spirit

This world

Watches over us/
sends us inspiration

You

3 How spiritual messages work

Master Ryuho Okawa, through his enlightenment, is capable of summoning any spirit from anywhere in the world, including the spirit world.

Master Okawa's way of receiving spiritual messages is fundamentally different from that of other psychic mediums who undergo trances and are thereby completely taken over by the spirits they are channeling.

Master Okawa's attainment of a high level of enlightenment enables him to retain full control of his consciousness and body throughout the duration of the spiritual message. To allow the spirits to express their own thoughts and personalities freely, however, Master Okawa usually softens the dominancy of his consciousness. This way, he is able to keep his own philosophies out of the way and ensure that the spiritual messages are pure expressions of the spirits he is channeling.

Since guardian spirits think at the same subconscious level as the person living on earth, Master Okawa can summon the spirit and find out what the person on earth is actually thinking. If the person has already returned to the other world, the spirit can give messages to the people living on earth through Master Okawa.

Since 2009, more than 1,000 sessions of spiritual messages have been openly recorded by Master Okawa, and the majority of these have been published. Spiritual messages from the guardian spirits of people living today such as U.S. President Donald Trump, Japanese Prime Minister Shinzo Abe and Chinese President Xi Jinping, as well as spiritual messages sent from the spirit world by Jesus Christ, Muhammad, Thomas Edison, Mother Teresa, Steve Jobs and Nelson Mandela are just a tiny pack of spiritual messages that were published so far.

Domestically, in Japan, these spiritual messages are being read by a wide range of politicians and mass media, and the high-level contents of these books are delivering an impact even more on politics, news and public opinion. In recent years, there have been spiritual messages recorded in English, and English translations are being done on the spiritual messages given in Japanese. These have been published overseas, one after another, and have started to shake the world.

1 The guardian spirit /
spirit in the other world...

2 Goes inside Master Okawa
in this world

3 Master Okawa speaks
the words of the guardian spirit /
spirit

*For more about spiritual messages and a complete list of books in the Spiritual Interview Series, visit **okawabooks.com***

ABOUT HAPPY SCIENCE

Happy Science is a global movement that empowers individuals to find purpose and spiritual happiness and to share that happiness with their families, societies, and the world. With more than twelve million members around the world, Happy Science aims to increase awareness of spiritual truths and expand our capacity for love, compassion, and joy so that together we can create the kind of world we all wish to live in.

Activities at Happy Science are based on the Principles of Happiness (Love, Wisdom, Self-Reflection, and Progress). These principles embrace worldwide philosophies and beliefs, transcending boundaries of culture and religions.

Love teaches us to give ourselves freely without expecting anything in return; it encompasses giving, nurturing, and forgiving.

Wisdom leads us to the insights of spiritual truths, and opens us to the true meaning of life and the will of God (the universe, the highest power, Buddha).

Self-Reflection brings a mindful, nonjudgmental lens to our thoughts and actions to help us find our truest selves—the essence of our souls—and deepen our connection to the highest power. It helps us attain a clean and peaceful mind and leads us to the right life path.

Progress emphasizes the positive, dynamic aspects of our spiritual growth—actions we can take to manifest and spread happiness around the world. It's a path that not only expands our soul growth, but also furthers the collective potential of the world we live in.

PROGRAMS AND EVENTS

The doors of Happy Science are open to all. We offer a variety of programs and events, including self-exploration and self-growth programs, spiritual seminars, meditation and contemplation sessions, study groups, and book events.

Our programs are designed to:
* Deepen your understanding of your purpose and meaning in life
* Improve your relationships and increase your capacity to love unconditionally
* Attain peace of mind, decrease anxiety and stress, and feel positive
* Gain deeper insights and a broader perspective on the world
* Learn how to overcome life's challenges
  ... and much more.

*For more information, visit **happy-science.org**.*

OUR ACTIVITIES

Happy Science does other various activities to provide support for those in need.

◆ **You Are An Angel! General Incorporated Association**
Happy Science has a volunteer network in Japan that encourages and supports children with disabilities as well as their parents and guardians.

◆ **Never Mind School for Truancy**
At 'Never Mind,' we support students who find it very challenging to attend schools in Japan. We also nurture their self-help spirit and power to rebound against obstacles in life based on Master Okawa's teachings and faith.

◆ **"Prevention Against Suicide" Campaign since 2003**
A nationwide campaign to reduce suicides; over 20,000 people commit suicide every year in Japan. "The Suicide Prevention Website-Words of Truth for You-" presents spiritual prescriptions for worries such as depression, lost love, extramarital affairs, bullying and work-related problems, thereby saving many lives.

◆ **Support for Anti-bullying Campaigns**
Happy Science provides support for a group of parents and guardians, Network to Protect Children from Bullying, a general incorporated foundation launched in Japan to end bullying, including those that can even be called a criminal offense. So far, the network received more than 5,000 cases and resolved 90% of them.

◆ The Golden Age Scholarship

This scholarship is granted to students who can contribute greatly and bring a hopeful future to the world.

◆ Success No.1
Buddha's Truth Afterschool Academy

Happy Science has over 180 classrooms throughout Japan and in several cities around the world that focus on afterschool education for children. The education focuses on faith and morals in addition to supporting children's school studies.

◆ Angel Plan V

For children under the age of kindergarten, Happy Science holds classes for nurturing healthy, positive, and creative boys and girls.

◆ Future Stars Training Department

The Future Stars Training Department was founded within the Happy Science Media Division with the goal of nurturing talented individuals to become successful in the performing arts and entertainment industry.

◆ New Star Production Co., Ltd.
ARI Production Co., Ltd.

We have companies to nurture actors and actresses, artists, and vocalists. They are also involved in film production.

DOCUMENTARY MOVIE
HEART TO HEART

In this documentary movie, Happy Science University students visit these NPO activities to discover what salvation truly is, and on the meaning of life, through heart to heart interviews.

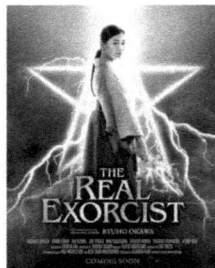

Lineup of Happy Science Movies

Discover the spiritual world you have never seen and
Come close to the Heart of God through these movies.

1994

+ **The Terrifying Revelations
of Nostradamus**
(live action)

1997

+ **Love Blows Like the Wind**
(animation)

2000

+ **The Laws of the Sun**
(animation)

2003

+ **The Golden Laws**
(animation)

2006

+ **The Laws of Eternity**
(animation)

2009

+ **The Rebirth of Buddha**
(animation)

2012

+ **The Final Judgement**
(live action)

+ **The Mystical Laws**
(animation)

2015

+ **The Laws of the Universe
- Part 0**
(animation)

2016

+ **I'm Fine, My Angel**
(live action)

2017

+ **The World We Live In**
(live action)

2018

+ **Heart to Heart**
(documentary)

+ **DAYBREAK**
(live action)

+ **The Laws of the Universe
- Part I**
(animation)

2019

+ **The Last White Witch**
(live action)

+ **Life is Beautiful
- Heart to Heart 2 -**
(documentary)

+ **Immortal Hero**
(live action)

- Coming soon -

2020

+ **The Real Exorcist**
(live action)

+ **Kiseki to no Deai
- Kokoro ni Yorisou 3 -**
(lit. Encounters with Miracles
- Heart to Heart 3 -)
(documentary)

+ **Twiceborn**
(live action)

˙Contact your nearest local branch for more information on how to watch HS movies.

CONTACT INFORMATION

Happy Science is a worldwide organization with faith centers around the globe. For a comprehensive list of centers, visit the worldwide directory at *happy-science.org*. The following are some of the many Happy Science locations:

UNITED STATES AND CANADA

New York
79 Franklin St., New York, NY 10013
Phone: 212-343-7972
Fax: 212-343-7973
Email: ny@happy-science.org
Website: happyscience-na.org

New Jersey
725 River Rd, #102B, Edgewater, NJ 07020
Phone: 201-313-0127
Fax: 201-313-0120
Email: nj@happy-science.org
Website: happyscience-na.org

Florida
5208 8th St., St. Zephyrhills, FL 33542
Phone: 813-715-0000
Fax: 813-715-0010
Email: florida@happy-science.org
Website: happyscience-na.org

Atlanta
1874 Piedmont Ave., NE Suite 360-C
Atlanta, GA 30324
Phone: 404-892-7770
Email: atlanta@happy-science.org
Website: happyscience-na.org

San Francisco
525 Clinton St.
Redwood City, CA 94062
Phone & Fax: 650-363-2777
Email: sf@happy-science.org
Website: happyscience-na.org

Los Angeles
1590 E. Del Mar Blvd., Pasadena, CA 91106
Phone: 626-395-7775
Fax: 626-395-7776
Email: la@happy-science.org
Website: happyscience-na.org

Orange County
10231 Slater Ave., #204
Fountain Valley, CA 92708
Phone: 714-745-1140
Email: oc@happy-science.org
Website: happyscience-na.org

San Diego
7841 Balboa Ave., Suite #202
San Diego, CA 92111
Phone: 619-381-7615
Fax: 626-395-7776
E-mail: sandiego@happy-science.org
Website: happyscience-na.org

Hawaii
Phone: 808-591-9772
Fax: 808-591-9776
Email: hi@happy-science.org
Website: happyscience-na.org

Kauai
3343 Kanakolu Street, Suite 5
Lihue, HI 96766, U.S.A.
Phone: 808-822-7007
Fax: 808-822-6007
Email: kauai-hi@happy-science.org
Website: kauai.happyscience-na.org

Toronto

845 The Queensway
Etobicoke ON M8Z 1N6 Canada
Phone: 1-416-901-3747
Email: toronto@happy-science.org
Website: happy-science.ca

Vancouver

#201-2607 East 49th Avenue
Vancouver, BC, V5S 1J9, Canada
Phone: 1-604-437-7735
Fax: 1-604-437-7764
Email: vancouver@happy-science.org
Website: happy-science.ca

INTERNATIONAL

Tokyo

1-6-7 Togoshi, Shinagawa
Tokyo, 142-0041 Japan
Phone: 81-3-6384-5770
Fax: 81-3-6384-5776
Email: tokyo@happy-science.org
Website: happy-science.org

Seoul

74, Sadang-ro 27-gil,
Dongjak-gu, Seoul, Korea
Phone: 82-2-3478-8777
Fax: 82-2-3478-9777
Email: korea@happy-science.org
Website: happyscience-korea.org

London

3 Margaret St.
London, W1W 8RE United Kingdom
Phone: 44-20-7323-9255
Fax: 44-20-7323-9344
Email: eu@happy-science.org
Website: happyscience-uk.org

Taipei

No. 89, Lane 155, Dunhua N. Road
Songshan District, Taipei City 105, Taiwan
Phone: 886-2-2719-9377
Fax: 886-2-2719-5570
Email: taiwan@happy-science.org
Website: happyscience-tw.org

Sydney

516 Pacific Hwy, Lane Cove North,
NSW 2066, Australia
Phone: 61-2-9411-2877
Fax: 61-2-9411-2822
Email: sydney@happy-science.org

Malaysia

No 22A, Block 2, Jalil Link Jalan Jalil Jaya 2,
Bukit Jalil 57000, Kuala Lumpur, Malaysia
Phone: 60-3-8998-7877
Fax: 60-3-8998-7977
Email: malaysia@happy-science.org
Website: happyscience.org.my

Brazil Headquarters

Rua Domingos de Morais 1154,
Vila Mariana, Sao Paulo SP
CEP 04009-002, Brazil
Phone: 55-11-5088-3800
Fax: 55-11-5088-3806
Email: sp@happy-science.org
Website: happyscience.com.br

Nepal

Kathmandu Metropolitan City Ward
No. 15,
Ring Road, Kimdol,
Sitapaila Kathmandu, Nepal
Phone: 97-714-272931
Email: nepal@happy-science.org

Jundiai

Rua Congo, 447, Jd. Bonfiglioli
Jundiai-CEP, 13207-340
Phone: 55-11-4587-5952
Email: jundiai@happy-science.org

Uganda

Plot 877 Rubaga Road, Kampala
P.O. Box 34130, Kampala, Uganda
Phone: 256-79-3238-002
Email: uganda@happy-science.org
Website: happyscience-uganda.org

HAPPINESS REALIZATION PARTY

The Happiness Realization Party (HRP) was founded in May 2009 by Master Ryuho Okawa as part of the Happy Science Group to offer concrete and proactive solutions to the current issues such as military threats from North Korea and China and the long-term economic recession. HRP aims to implement drastic reforms of the Japanese government, thereby bringing peace and prosperity to Japan. To accomplish this, HRP proposes two key policies:

1) Strengthening the national security and the Japan-U.S. alliance which plays a vital role in the stability of Asia.

2) Improving the Japanese economy by implementing drastic tax cuts, taking monetary easing measures and creating new major industries.

HRP advocates that Japan should offer a model of a religious nation that allows diverse values and beliefs to coexist, and that contributes to global peace.

*For more information, visit **en.hr-party.jp***

ABOUT IRH PRESS

IRH Press Co., Ltd., based in Tokyo, was founded in 1987 as a publishing division of Happy Science. IRH Press publishes religious and spiritual books, journals, magazines and also operates broadcast and film production enterprises. For more information, visit *okawabooks.com*.

Follow us on:

Facebook: Okawa Books   **Twitter**: Okawa Books
Goodreads: Ryuho Okawa   **Instagram**: OkawaBooks
Pinterest: Okawa Books

RYUHO OKAWA'S LAWS SERIES

The Laws Series is an annual volume of books that are mainly comprised of Ryuho Okawa's lectures on various topics that highlight principles and guidelines for the activities of Happy Science every year. *The Laws of the Sun*, the first publication of the Laws Series, published in 1987. Since then, all of the Laws Series' titles have ranked in the annual best-selling list for more than two decades, setting socio-cultural trends in Japan and around the world.

THE TRILOGY

The first three volumes of the Laws Series, *The Laws of the Sun*, *The Golden Laws*, and *The Nine Dimensions* make a trilogy that completes the basic framework of the teachings of God's Truths. *The Laws of the Sun* discusses the structure of God's Laws, *The Golden Laws* expounds on the doctrine of time, and *The Nine Dimensions* reveals the nature of space.

BOOKS BY RYUHO OKAWA

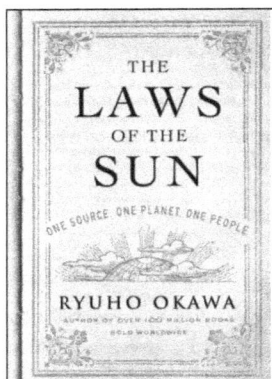

THE LAWS OF THE SUN
ONE SOURCE, ONE PLANET, ONE PEOPLE

Paperback • 288 pages • $15.95
ISBN: 978-1-942125-43-3

IMAGINE IF YOU COULD ASK GOD why He created this world and what spiritual laws He used to shape us—and everything around us. If we could understand His designs and intentions, we could discover what our goals in life should be and whether our actions move us closer to those goals or farther away.

At a young age, a spiritual calling prompted Ryuho Okawa to outline what he innately understood to be universal truths for all humankind. In *The Laws of the Sun*, Okawa outlines these laws of the universe and provides a road map for living one's life with greater purpose and meaning.

In this powerful book, Ryuho Okawa reveals the transcendent nature of consciousness and the secrets of our multidimensional universe and our place in it. By understanding the different stages of love and following the Buddhist Eightfold Path, he believes we can speed up our eternal process of development. *The Laws of the Sun* shows the way to realize true happiness—a happiness that continues from this world through the other.

---

*For a complete list of books, visit **okawabooks.com***

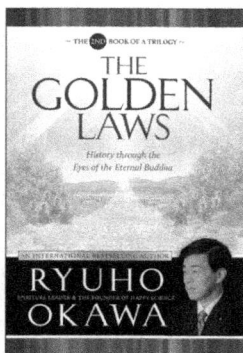

THE GOLDEN LAWS
HISTORY THROUGH THE EYES OF THE ETERNAL BUDDHA

Paperback • 201 pages • $14.95
ISBN: 978-1-941779-81-1

Throughout history, Great Guiding Spirits of Light have been present on Earth in both the East and the West at crucial points in human history to further our spiritual development. *The Golden Laws* reveals how Divine Plan has been unfolding on Earth, and outlines 5,000 years of the secret history of humankind. Once we understand the true course of history, through the past, the present and into the future, we cannot help but become aware of the significance of our spiritual mission in the present age.

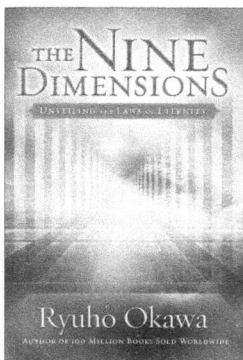

THE NINE DIMENSIONS
UNVEILING THE LAWS OF ETERNITY

Paperback • 168 pages • $15.95
ISBN: 978-0-982698-56-3

This book is a window into the mind of our loving God, who designed this world and the vast, wondrous world of our afterlife as a school with many levels through which our souls learn and grow. When the religions and cultures of the world discover the truth of their common spiritual origin, they will be inspired to accept their differences, come together under faith in God, and build an era of harmony and peaceful progress on Earth.

*For a complete list of books, visit **okawabooks.com***

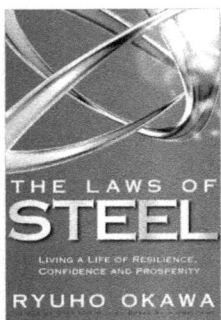

THE LAWS OF STEEL

LIVING A LIFE OF RESILIENCE,
CONFIDENCE AND PROSPERITY

Paperback • 264 pages • $16.95
ISBN: 978-1-942125-65-5

This book is a compilation of six lectures that Ryuho Okawa gave in 2018 and 2019, each containing passionate messages for us to open a brighter future. This powerful and inspiring book will not only show us the ways to achieve true happiness and prosperity, but also the ways to solve many global issues we now face.

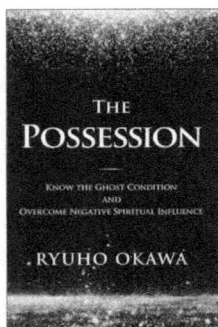

THE POSSESSION

KNOW THE GHOST CONDITION AND OVERCOME
NEGATIVE SPIRITUAL INFLUENCE

Paperback • 114 pages • $14.95
ISBN: 978-1-943869-66-4

Possession is neither an exceptional occurrence nor unscientific superstition; it's a phenomenon, based on spiritual principles, that is still quite common in the modern society. Through this book, you can find the way to change your own mind and free yourself from possession, and the way to exorcise devils by relying on the power of angels and God.

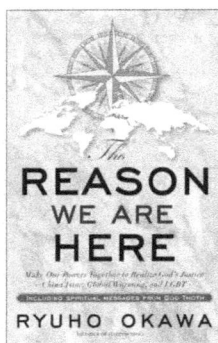

THE REASON WE ARE HERE

MAKE OUR POWERS TOGETHER TO REALIZE
GOD'S JUSTICE -CHINA ISSUE, GLOBAL
WARMING, AND LGBT-

Paperback • 215 pages • $14.95
ISBN: 978-1-943869-62-6

The Reason We Are Here is a book of thought that is unlike any other: its global perspective, timely opinion on current issues, and spiritual class are unmatched. The main content is the lecture in Toronto, Canada given in October 2019 by Ryuho Okawa, a Japanese spiritual leader and the national teacher of Japan.

---

*For a complete list of books, visit **okawabooks.com***

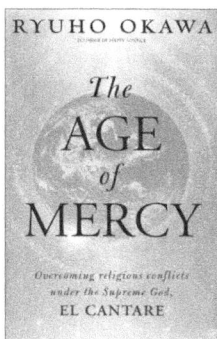

THE AGE OF MERCY

OVERCOMING RELIGIOUS CONFLICTS UNDER THE SUPREME GOD, EL CANTARE

Hardcover • 110 pages • $22.95
ISBN: 978-1-943869-51-0

Why are there conflicts in the world? How can people understand each other better? This book is a message from the Supreme God who has been guiding humankind from the beginning of creation.

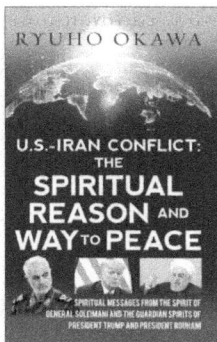

U.S.-IRAN CONFLICT: THE SPIRITUAL REASON AND WAY TO PEACE

SPIRITUAL MESSAGES FROM THE SPIRIT OF GENERAL SOLEIMANI AND THE GUARDIAN SPIRITS OF PRESIDENT TRUMP AND PRESIDENT ROUHANI

Paperback • 226 pages • $13.95
ISBN: 978-1-943869-68-8

Through these spiritual interviews, you will know that the U.S.-Iran conflict is essentially a religious conflict between Christianity and Islam, and that this book offers a possible solution.

UFOS CAUGHT ON CAMERA!

A SPIRITUAL INVESTIGATION ON VIDEOS AND PHOTOS OF THE LUMINOUS OBJECTS VISITING EARTH

Paperback • 112 pages • $17.95
ISBN: 978-1-943869-31-2

In the Summer of 2018, over 60 types of UFOs appeared before the author. *UFOs Caught on Camera!* is a detailed compilation of Okawa's sightings, with visual analysis of the luminous objects visiting Earth and spiritually sourced commentary of the extraterrestrial intelligence behind them.

*For a complete list of books, visit **okawabooks.com***

THE NEW RESURRECTION
My Miraculous Story of Overcoming Illness and Death

THE ROYAL ROAD OF LIFE
Beginning Your Path of Inner Peace, Virtue, and a Life of Purpose

THE LAWS OF GREAT ENLIGHTENMENT
Always Walk with Buddha

I CAN
Discover Your Power Within

HONG KONG REVOLUTION
Spiritual Messages of the Guardian Spirits of Xi Jinping and
Agnes Chow Ting

WORRY-FREE LIVING
Let Go of Stress and Live in Peace and Happiness

THE STARTING POINT OF HAPPINESS
An Inspiring Guide to Positive Living with Faith, Love, and Courage

HEALING FROM WITHIN
Life-Changing Keys to Calm, Spiritual, and Healthy Living

SPIRITUAL INTERVIEW WITH
THE GUARDIAN SPIRIT OF NEW SOUTH
KOREAN PRESIDENT MOON JAE-IN
The True Intentions Behind His Korean Unification

---

*For a complete list of books, visit **okawabooks.com***